Draw BIRDS

David Brown

Series Editors: David and Brenda Herbert

A & C BLACK · LONDON

Reprinted 1982, 1985, 1989, 1993
by A & C Black (Publishers) Limited
35 Bedford Row, London WC1R 4JH

ISBN 0-7136-2250-4

First published 1980
by Pitman Publishing Ltd

Printed and bound in Great Britain
by Hollen Street Press, Berwick upon Tweed

Contents

Making a start

Learning to draw is largely a matter of practice and observation—so draw as much and as often as you can, and use your eyes all the time. The less you think about *how* you are drawing and the more you think about *what* you are drawing, the better your drawing will be.

The best equipment will not itself make you a better artist—a masterpiece can be drawn with a stump of pencil on a scrap of paper. But good equipment is encouraging and pleasant to use, so buy the best you can afford and don't be afraid to use it freely.

Experiment with the biggest piece of paper and the boldest, softest piece of chalk or crayon you can find, filling the paper with lines to get a feeling of freedom. Even if you think you have a gift for tiny delicate line drawings with a fine pen or pencil, this is worth trying. It will act as a 'loosening up' exercise. The results may surprise you.

Be self-critical. If a drawing looks wrong, scrap it and start again. A second, third or even fourth attempt will often be better than the first, because you are learning more about the subject all the time. Use an eraser as little as possible—piecemeal correction won't help. Don't re-trace your lines. If a line is right the first time, leave it alone—heavier re-drawing leads to a dull, mechanical look.

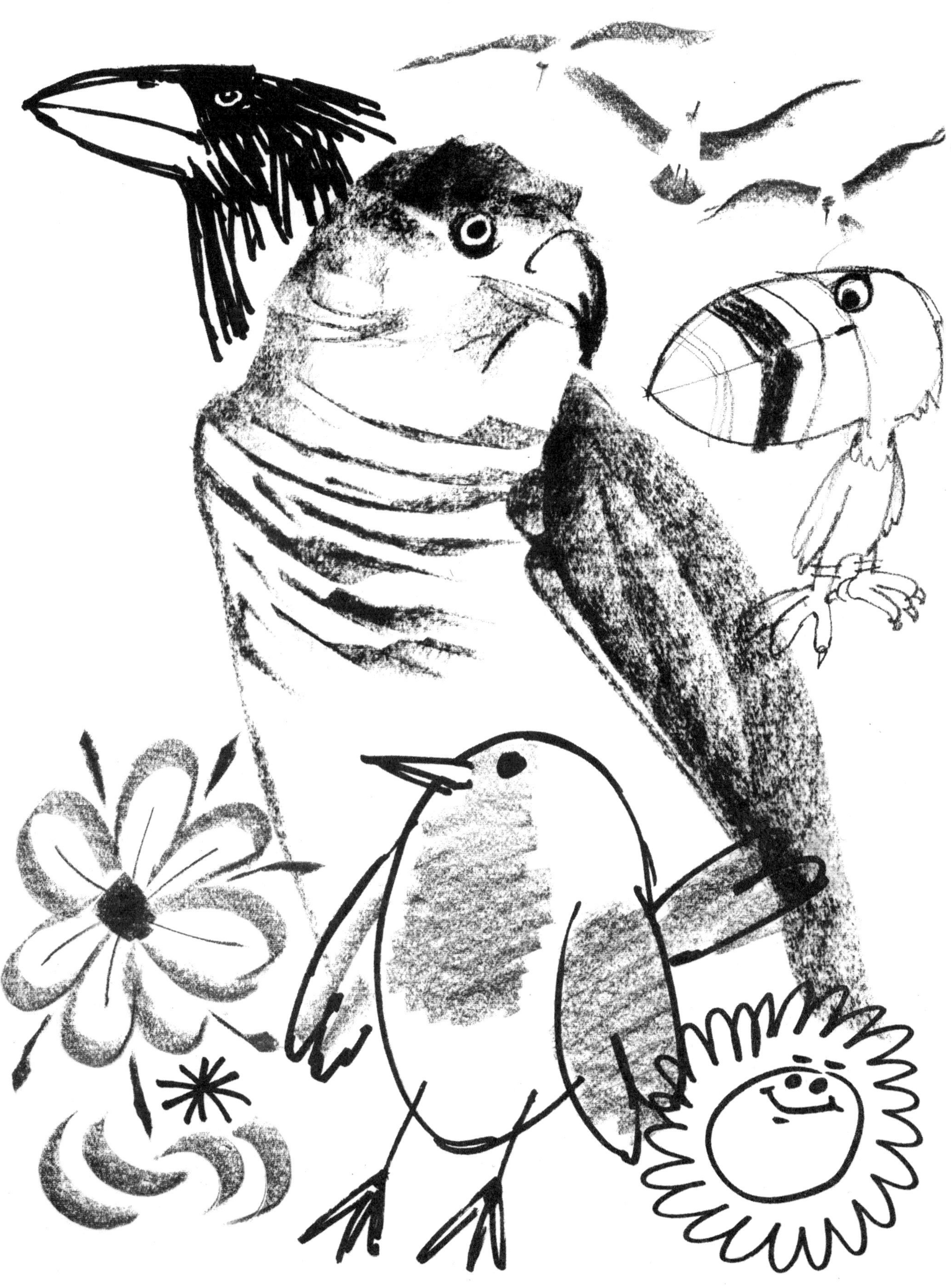

What to draw with

Pencils are graded according to hardness, from 6H (the hardest) through 5H, 4H, 3H, 2H to H; then HB, through B, 2B, 3B, 4B, 5B up to 6B (the softest). For most purposes, a soft pencil (HB or softer) is best. If you keep it sharp, it will draw as fine a line as a hard pencil but with less pressure, which makes it easier to control. Sometimes it is effective to smudge the line with your finger or an eraser, but if you do this too much the drawing will look woolly. A fine range of graphite drawing pencils is Royal Sovereign.

Charcoal (which is very soft) is excellent for large, bold sketches, but not for detail. If you use it, beware of accidental smudging. A drawing can even be dusted or rubbed off the paper altogether. To prevent this, spray with fixative. Charcoal pencils, such as the Royal Sovereign, are also very useful.

Pastels (available in a wide range of colours) are softer still. Since drawings in pastel are usually called 'paintings', they are really beyond the scope of this book.

Pens vary as much as pencils or crayons. The Gillott 659 is a very popular crowquill pen. Ink has a quality of its own, but of course it cannot be erased. Mapping pens are only suitable for delicate detail and minute cross-hatching.

Special artist's pens, such as the Gillott 303, or the Gillott 404, allow you a more varied line according to the angle at which you hold them and the pressure you use.

Reed, bamboo and quill pens are good for bold lines and you can make the nib end narrower or wider with the help of a sharp knife or razor blade. This kind of pen has to be dipped frequently into the ink.

Inks also vary. Waterproof Indian ink quickly clogs the pen. Pelikan Fount India, which is nearly as black, flows more smoothly and does not leave a varnishy deposit on the pen. Ordinary fountain-pen or writing inks (black, blue, green or brown) are not so opaque and give a drawing more variety of tone. You can mix water with ink to make it thinner, but for Indian ink use distilled or rain water because ordinary water will make it curdle.

Ball point pens make a drawing look a bit mechanical, but they are cheap and fool-proof and useful for quick notes.

Felt pens are useful for quick notes and sketches, but are not good for more elaborate and finished drawings.

Brushes are most versatile drawing instruments. The biggest sable brush has a fine point, and the smallest brush laid on its side provides a line broader than the broadest nib. You can add depth and variety to a pen or crayon drawing by washing over it with a brush dipped in clean water.

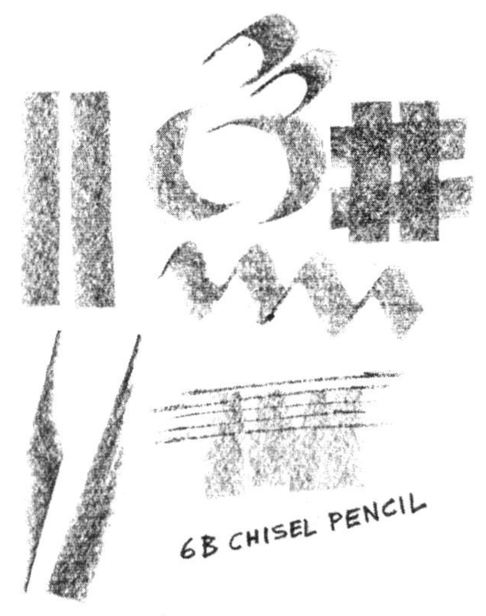

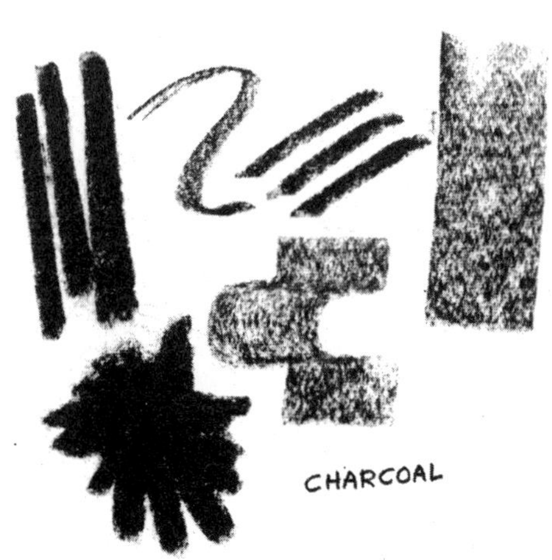

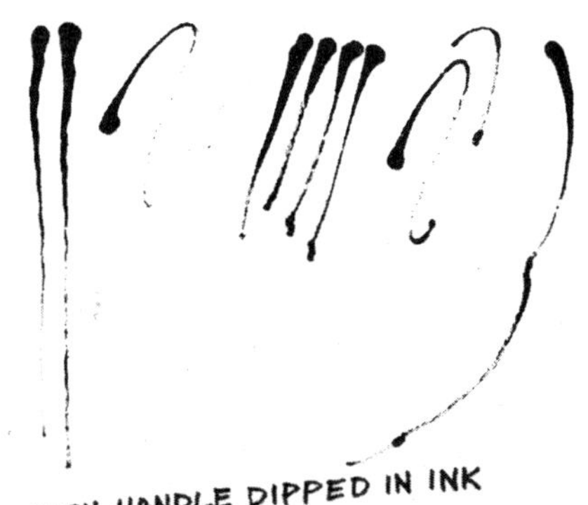

Mixed methods are often pleasing. Try making drawings with pen and pencil, pen and wax or wax crayon and wash. And try drawing with a pen on wet paper.

Experiment with various media. Discover their range and limitations. You will probably find that you prefer one to the others, so use it. If you don't enjoy your work, your enthusiasm will diminish. There's no point at this stage in struggling with a medium you don't like, but delay your decision until you have tried as many as possible. This does not mean that you should abandon all other media. When you have gained confidence with your chosen one, try the others again; you will be surprised what a little experience and confidence can do.

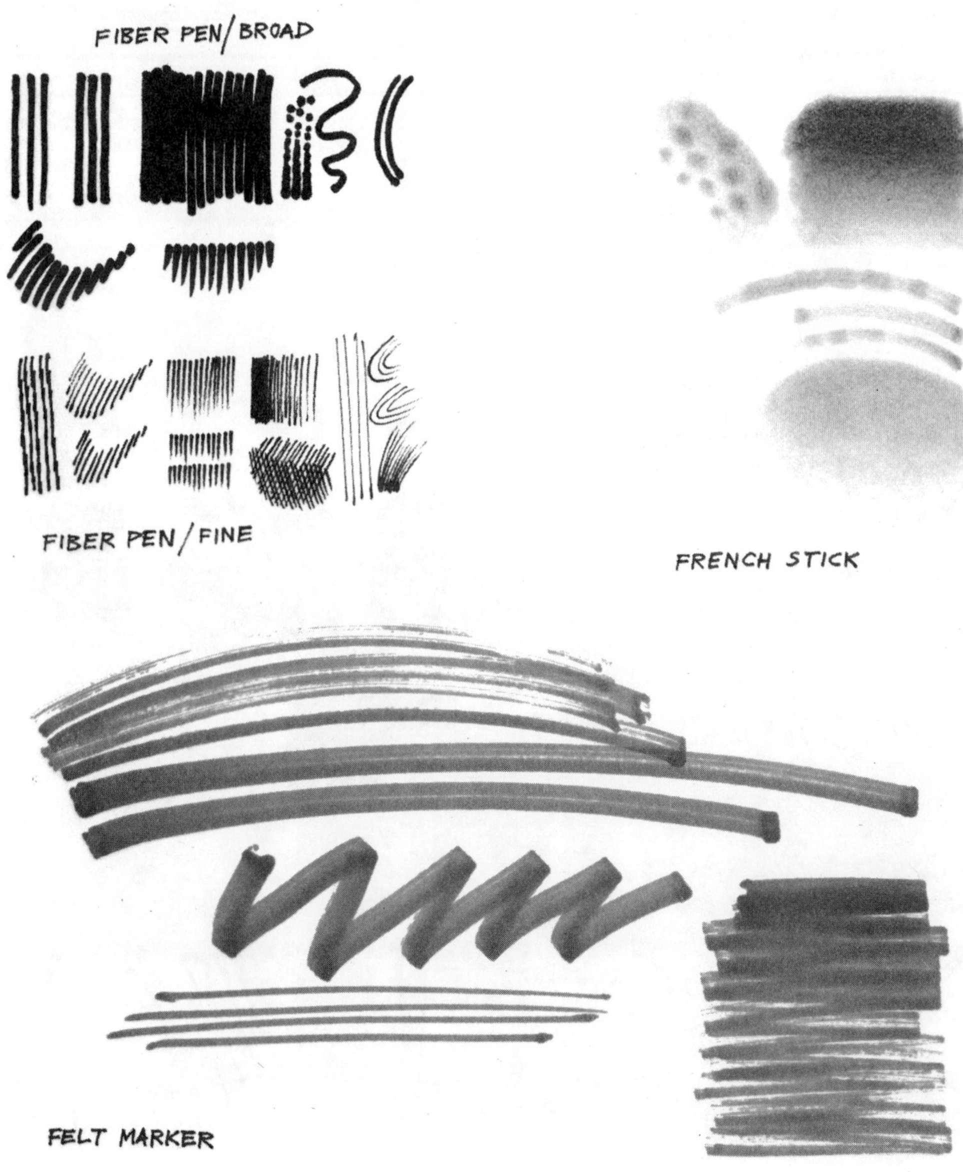

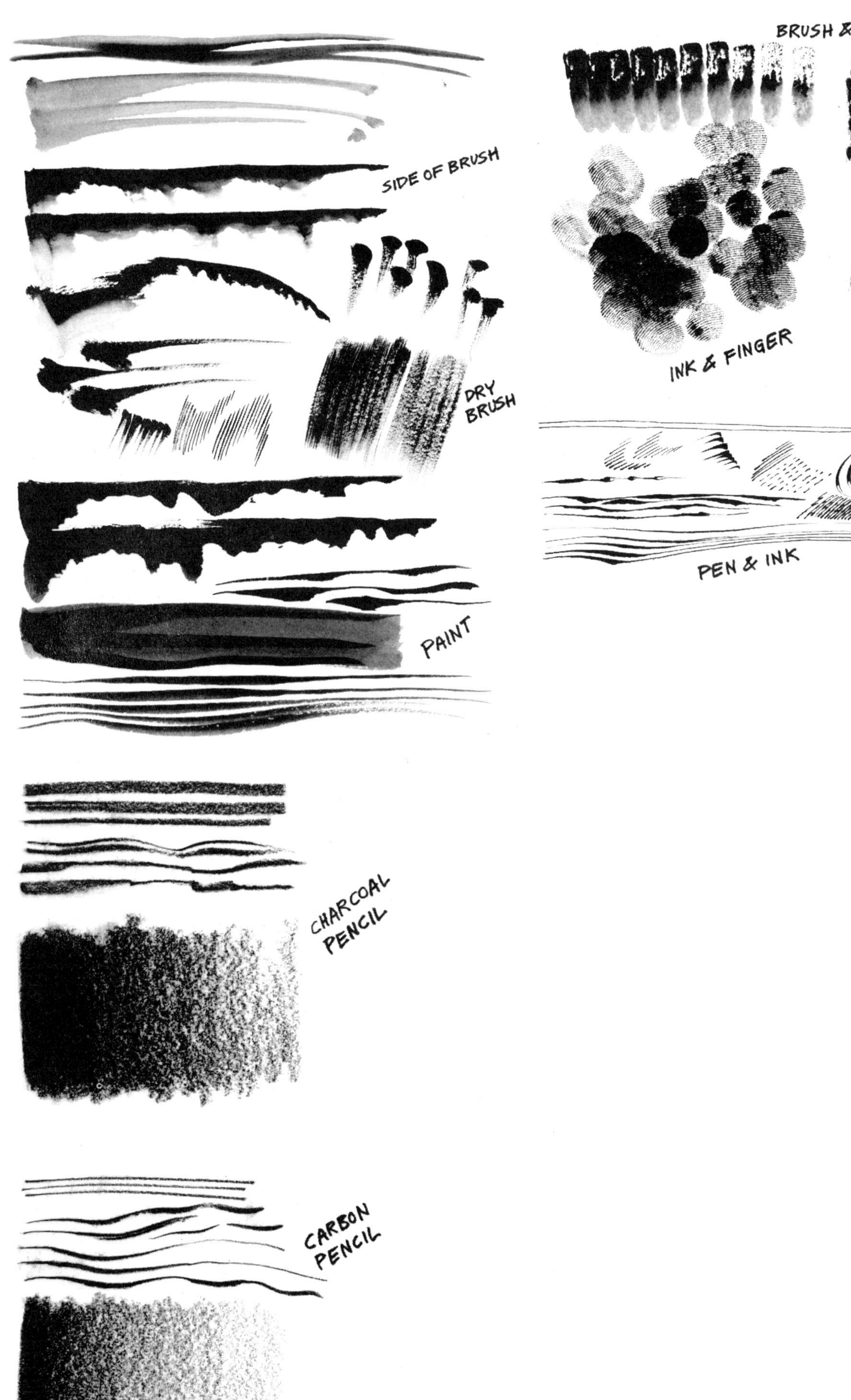
SIDE OF BRUSH
DRY BRUSH
PAINT
BRUSH & PAINT
INK & FINGER
PEN & INK
CHARCOAL PENCIL
CARBON PENCIL

Anatomy and shape

A basic knowledge of a bird's anatomy will help you understand its exterior shape. This drawing shows the bone structure. Take a close look at the next chicken you have for dinner, particularly if it is a fresh one, complete with head and claws. Study it before and after it is carved. Make detailed drawing notes—like these ones here, which show the varying shape of a claw brought about by the lifestyle of different birds.

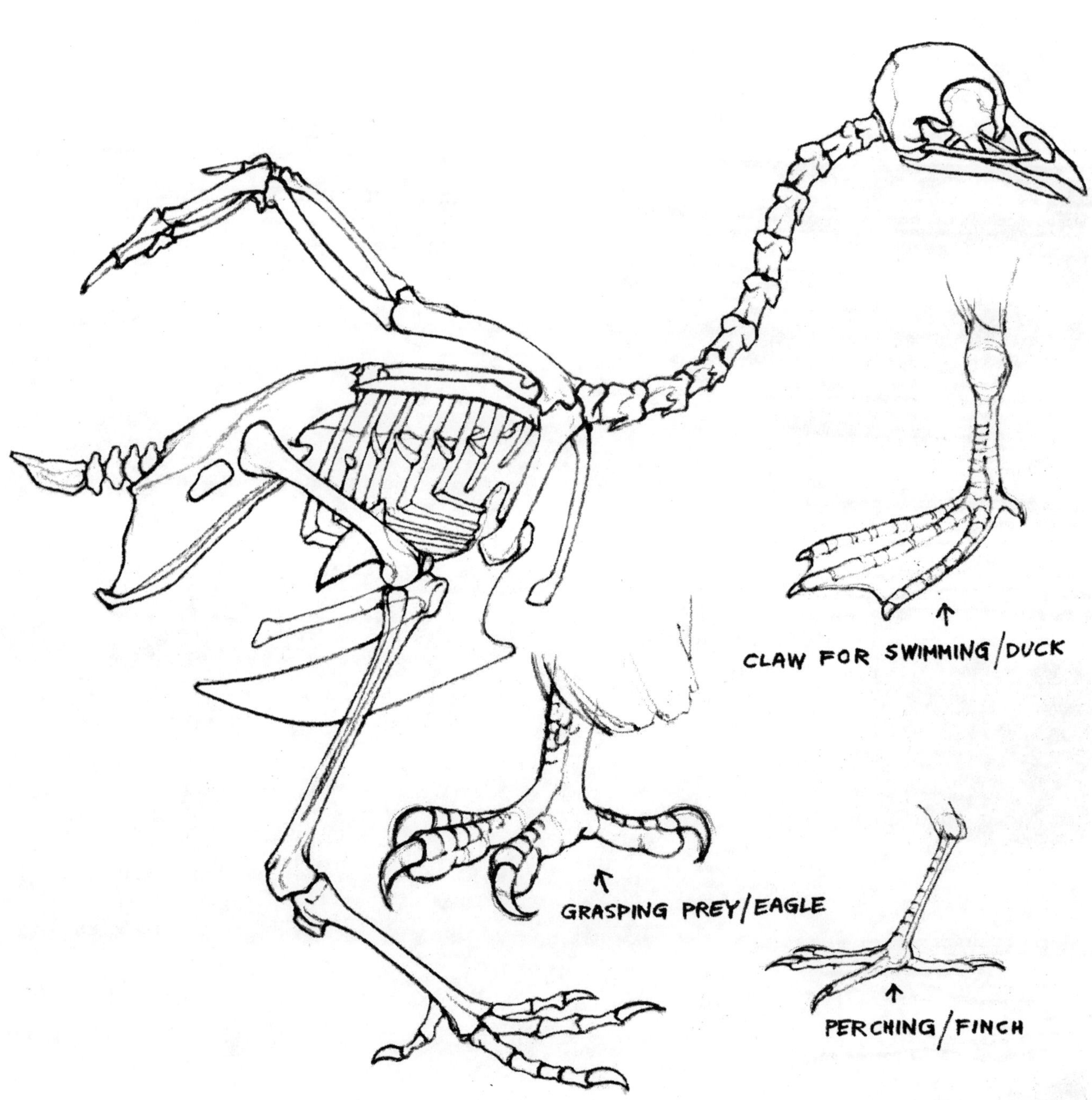

Study the various parts of the body, and again make detailed
drawing notes and sketches. Notice how the wing of a Swift
(left) differs·in shape from that of a Thrush (right) although
the construction is the same. Remember that tail feathers fold
so that the centre ones are on top and the outside ones
underneath, as in the diagram. The shape of each part of a
bird's beak, eye, neck, wing, tail, leg, claw varies according to
the needs of its environment and eating habits.

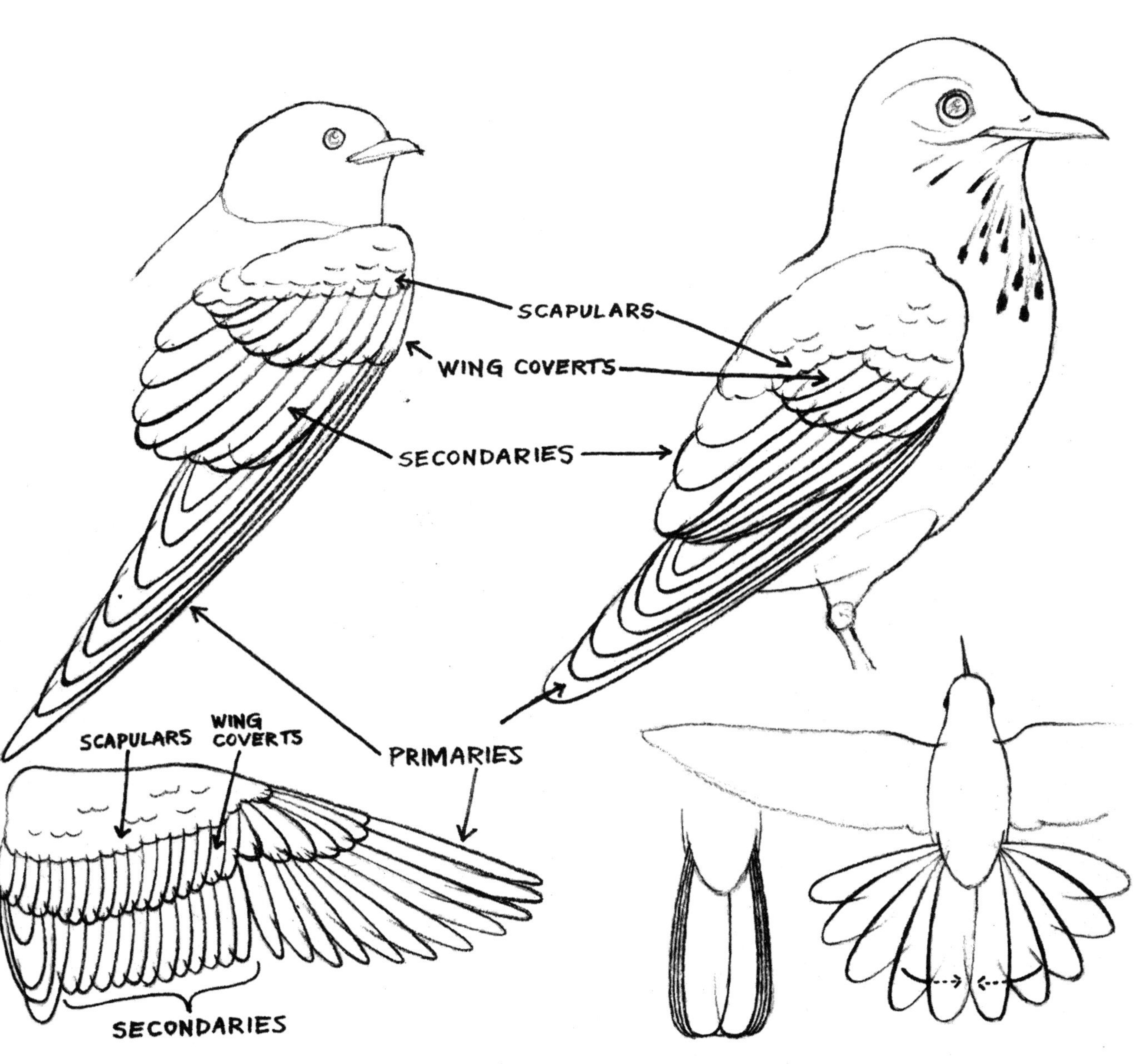

Heads come in many shapes. Notice the beak size of the Hornbill compared with that of the birds of prey below—who need a small curved beak to tear the flesh of their victims. The long, streamlined beak of the Kingfisher helps it to catch fish. Notice also the size of the eye in relation to the rest of the head. Flesh-eating birds need large, powerful eyes to see, from great distance, the small animals on which they live.

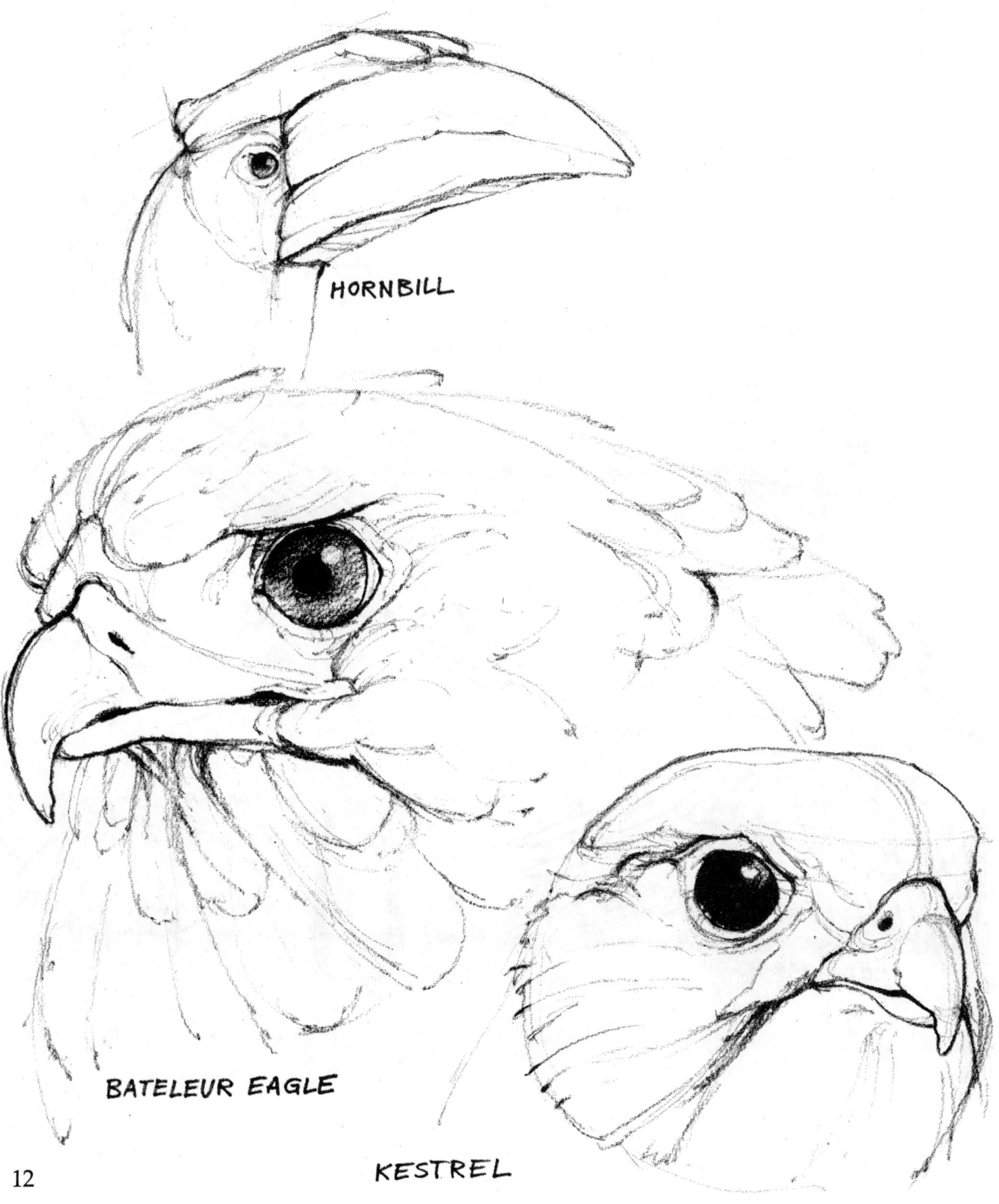

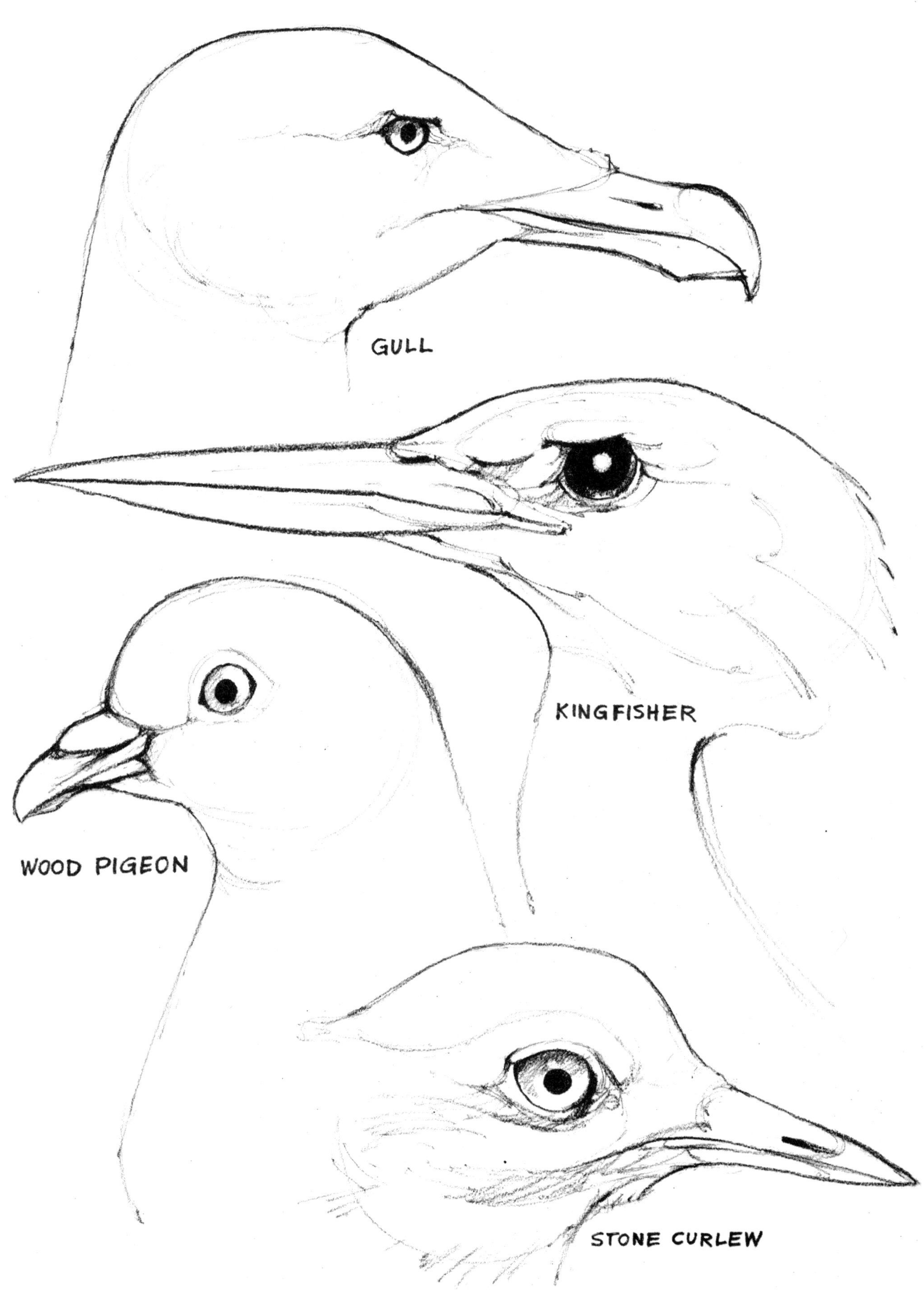
GULL
KINGFISHER
WOOD PIGEON
STONE CURLEW

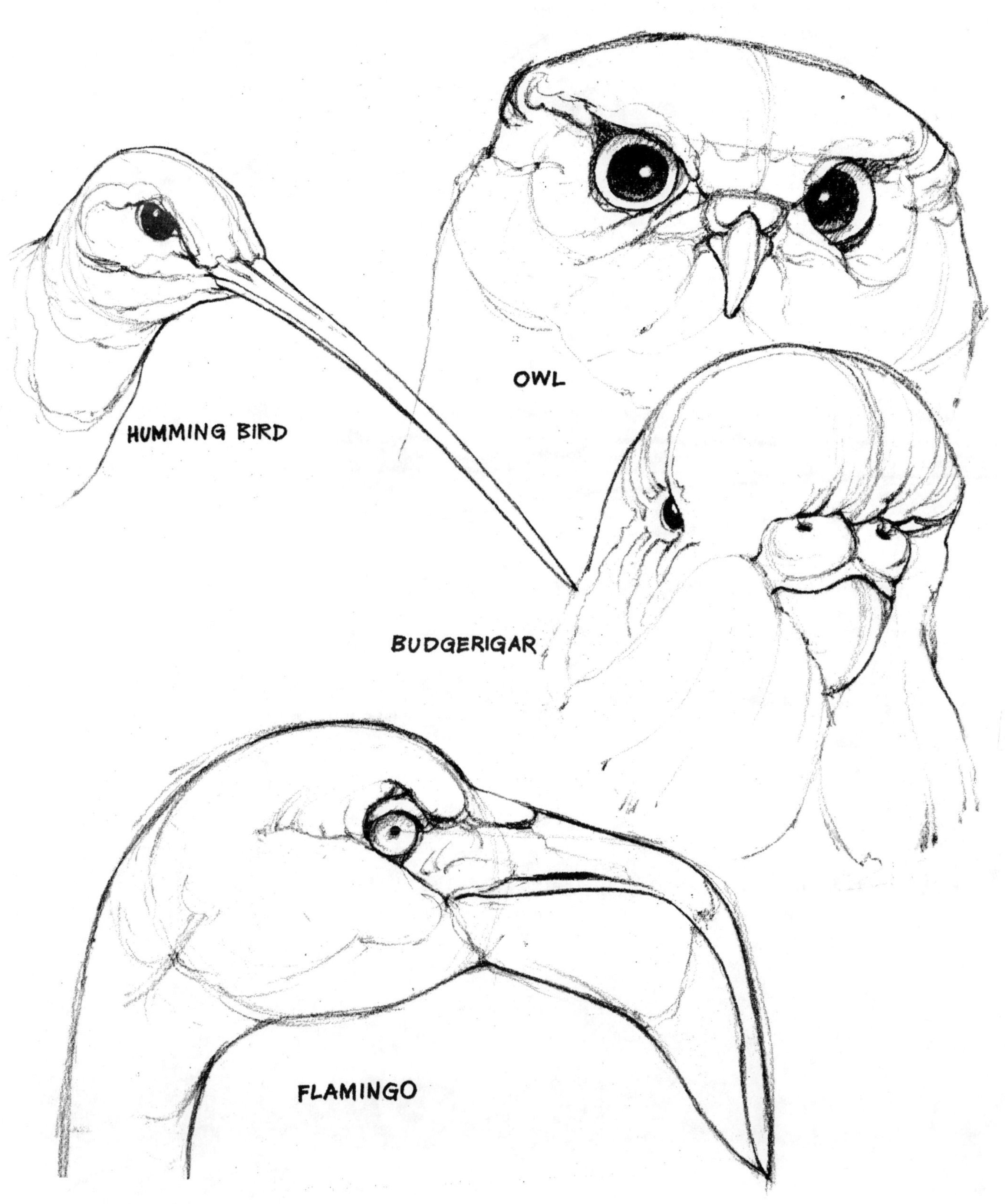

HUMMING BIRD
OWL
BUDGERIGAR
FLAMINGO

You can best capture the
expression and mood of
your subject by studying
the eyes. Compare the
penetrating gaze of an
Owl with the inquisitive
wide eyes of a Parrot.

While actually drawing,
go on comparing the
shapes and proportions
of the various parts.
Observe, for example,
whether the distance
between the base of the
beak and the eye of a
Blue Tit is equal to the
width of his eye.

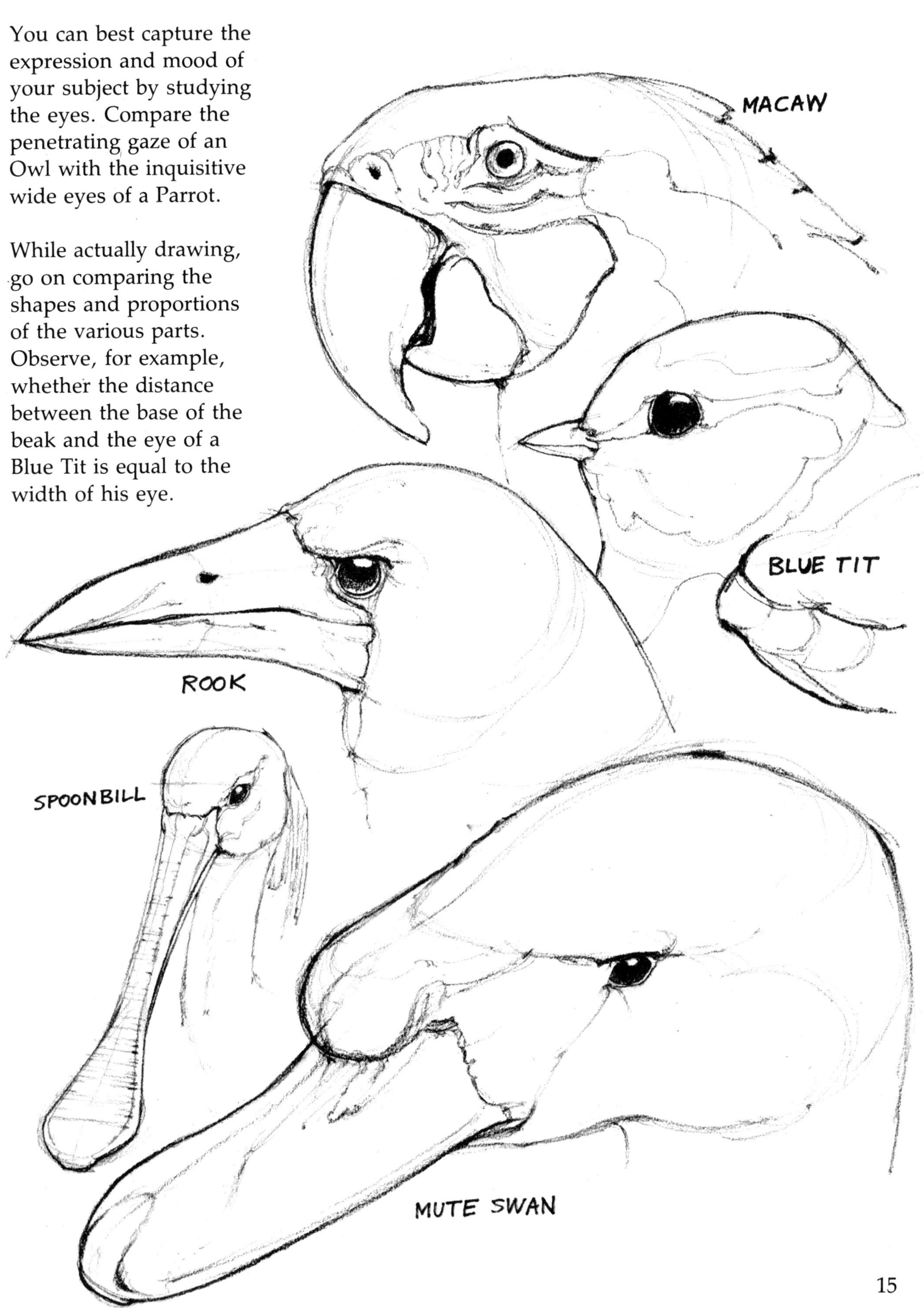

Proportion

The essence of good draughtsmanship is getting proportions correct. The most common mistake is getting them wrong. Try using the head as a unit of measure. Hold your pencil vertically at arm's length, with the top of the pencil in line with the top of the bird's head, as in the diagram. Use this measure to work out how many heads make up the bird's height, keeping your thumb on the same spot on the pencil and the pencil at arm's length.
This Seagull is six heads tall.

Now roughly draw the bird's head and, using this as your unit of measurement, mark out the number of heads you would need to get the correct height. Of course, you can use any other part of the body as a measuring unit. The length of this seagull, for example, was worked out by using the distance from the back of the head to the tip of the beak.

Practice in doing this will train your eye to *see* proportions correctly. Use photographs to start with, or better still visit a museum which has cases of stuffed birds.

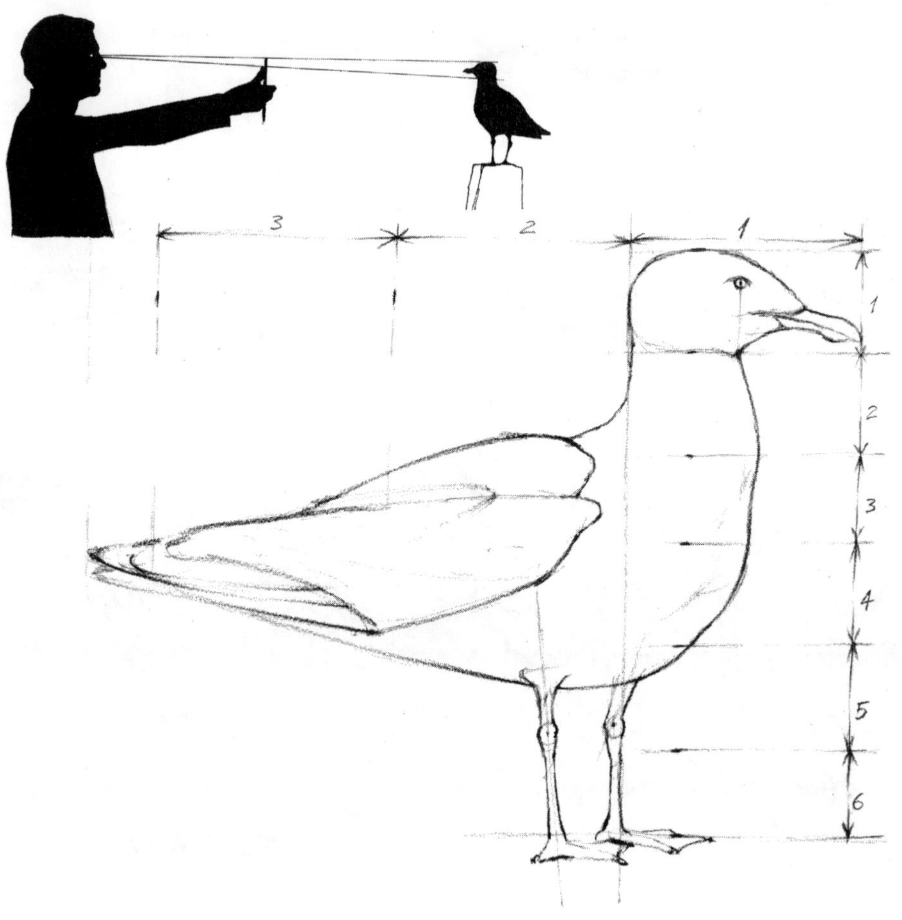

Study the shape of a bird carefully, noticing which parts of the
body line up and what angles are produced by the shape of
the body. Draw contour lines over various parts of the
anatomy to show the whole form.

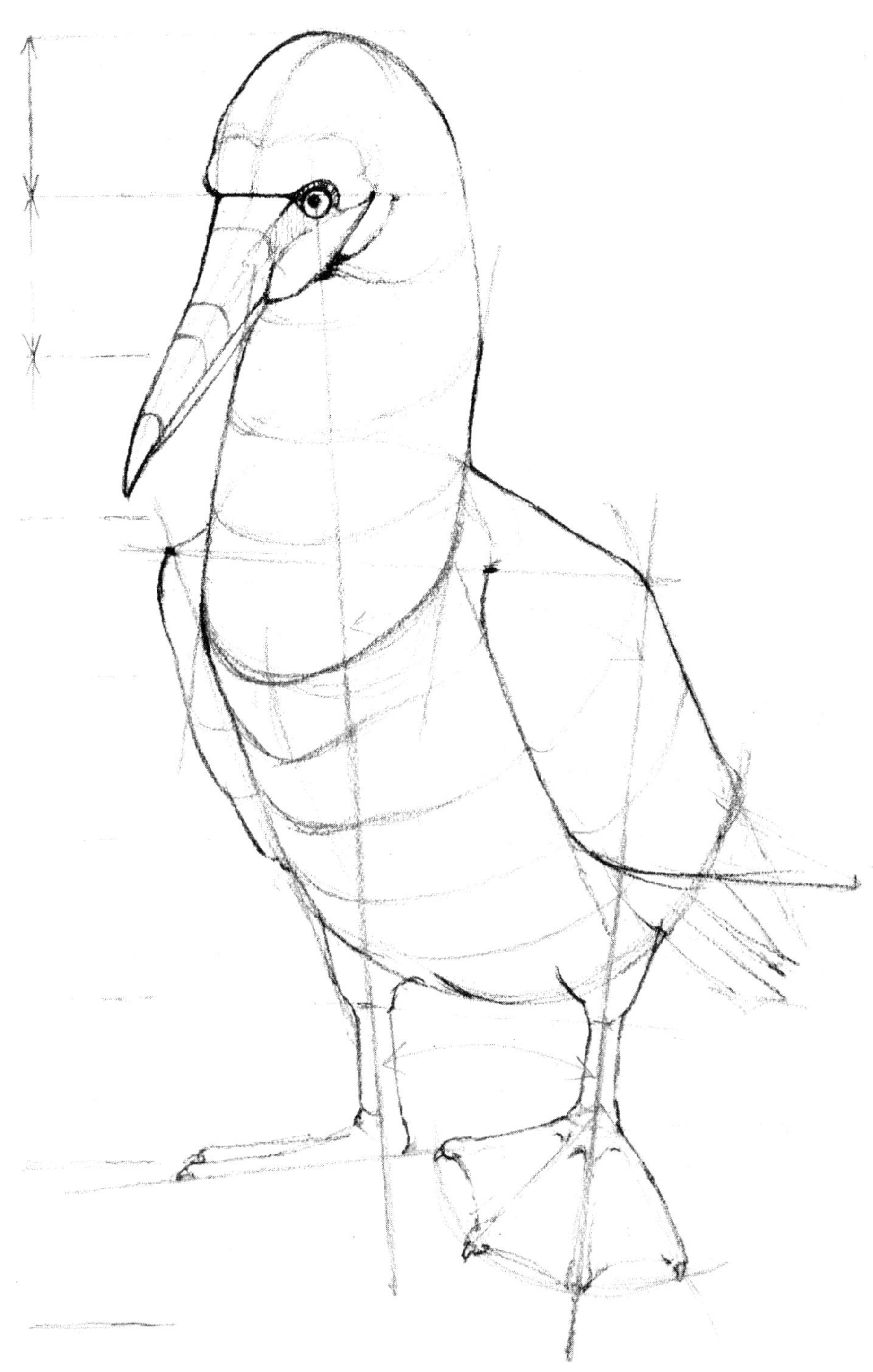

Basic shapes

When starting a drawing, try to see your subject in its simplest form. It helps to half-close your eyes. By doing so you shut out most of the detail, which allows you to concentrate on the basic shapes.

Notice how similar is the basic body shape of each of these long-legged birds.

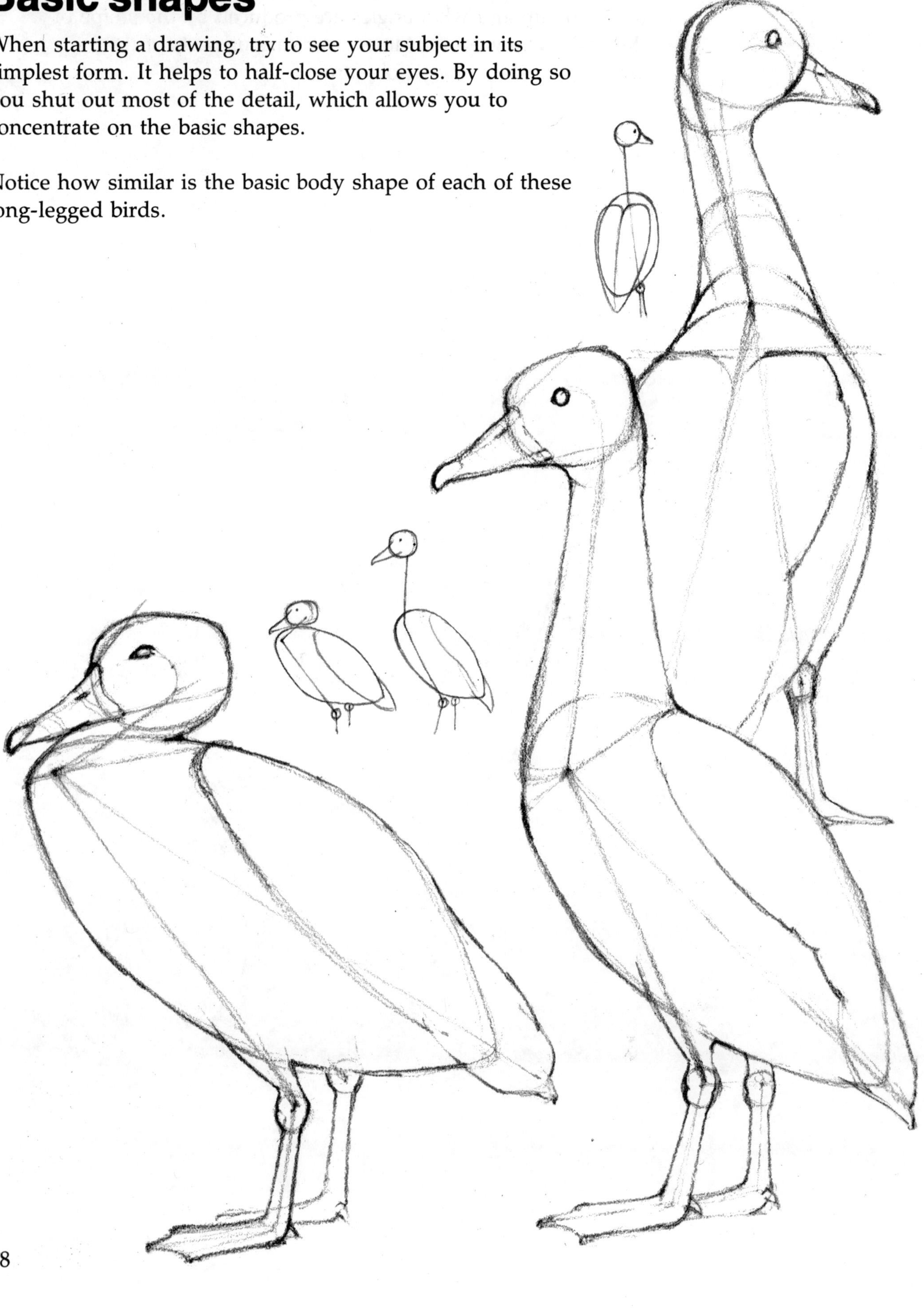

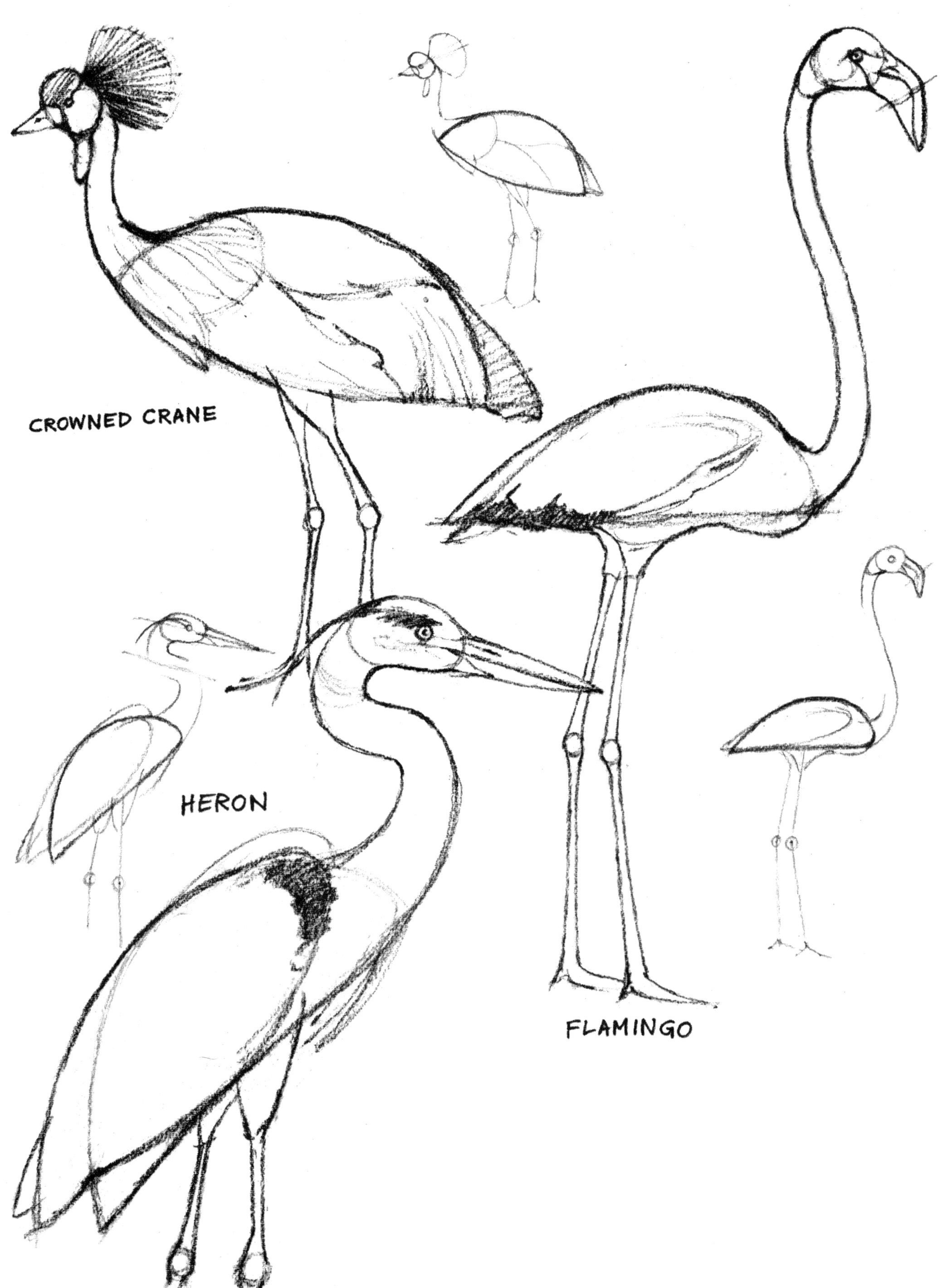

CROWNED CRANE
HERON
FLAMINGO

The Penguin makes a good model, because he will often hold a pose for several minutes. Take a sketching pad with you the next time you visit a zoo.

Little birds are not so obliging. You need a lot of patience to draw them from life, though a bird-table near a window will help.

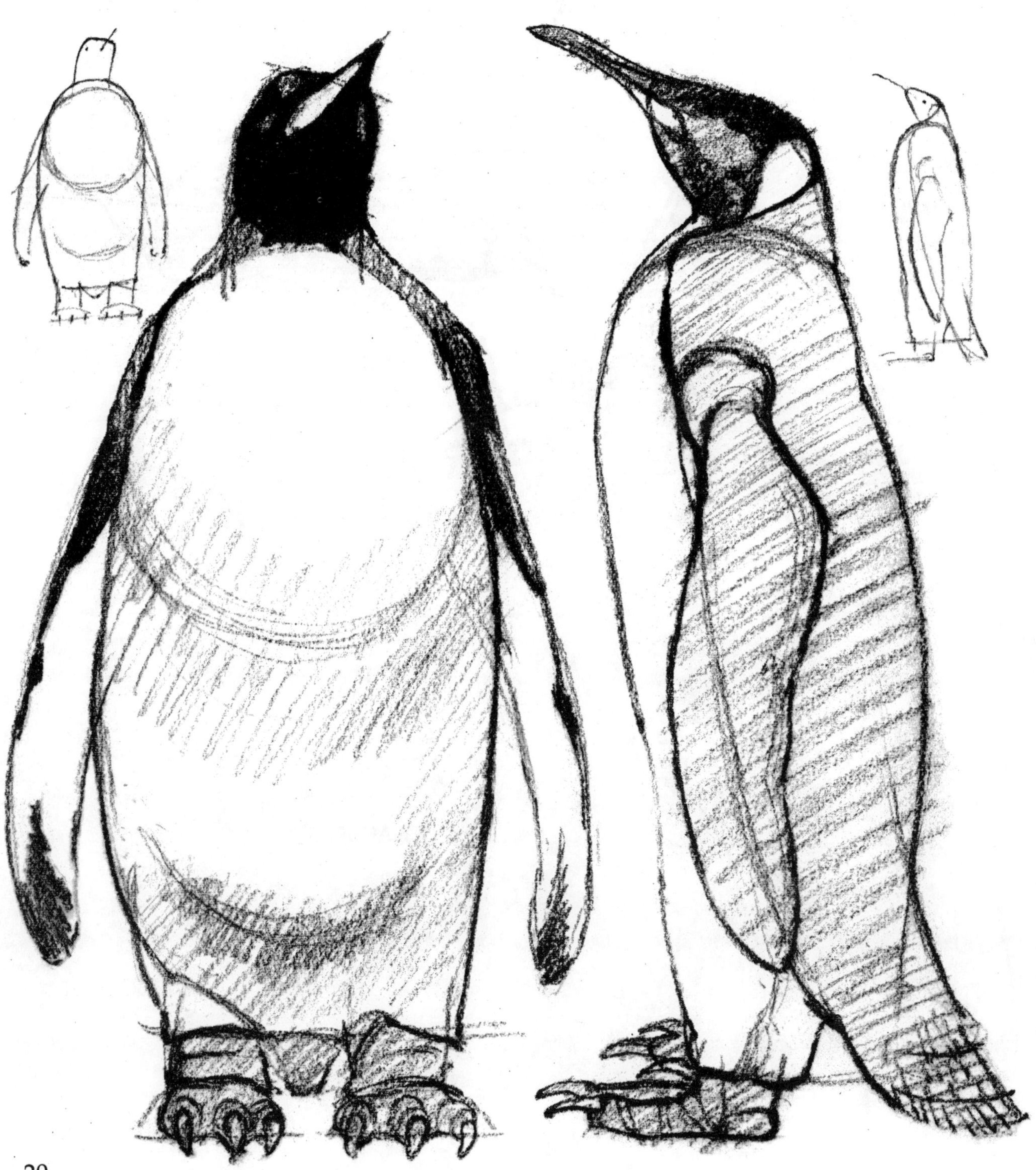

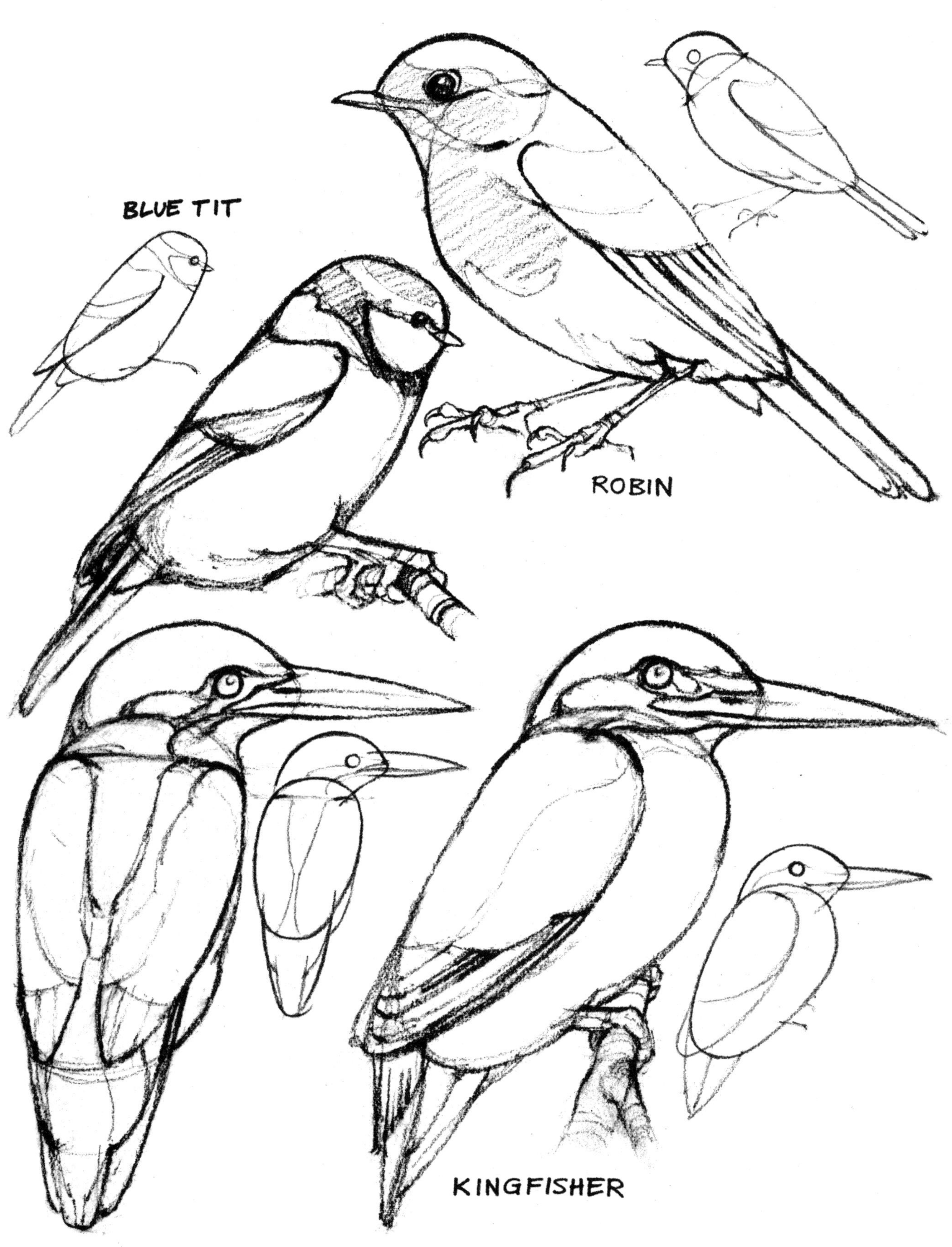

BLUE TIT
ROBIN
KINGFISHER

Construct your drawings; don't simply draw them in outline.
Notice how one part of a bird fits into the next. Look at the
size of its feet in relation to its head. Chickens need large,
strong feet for scratching the ground.

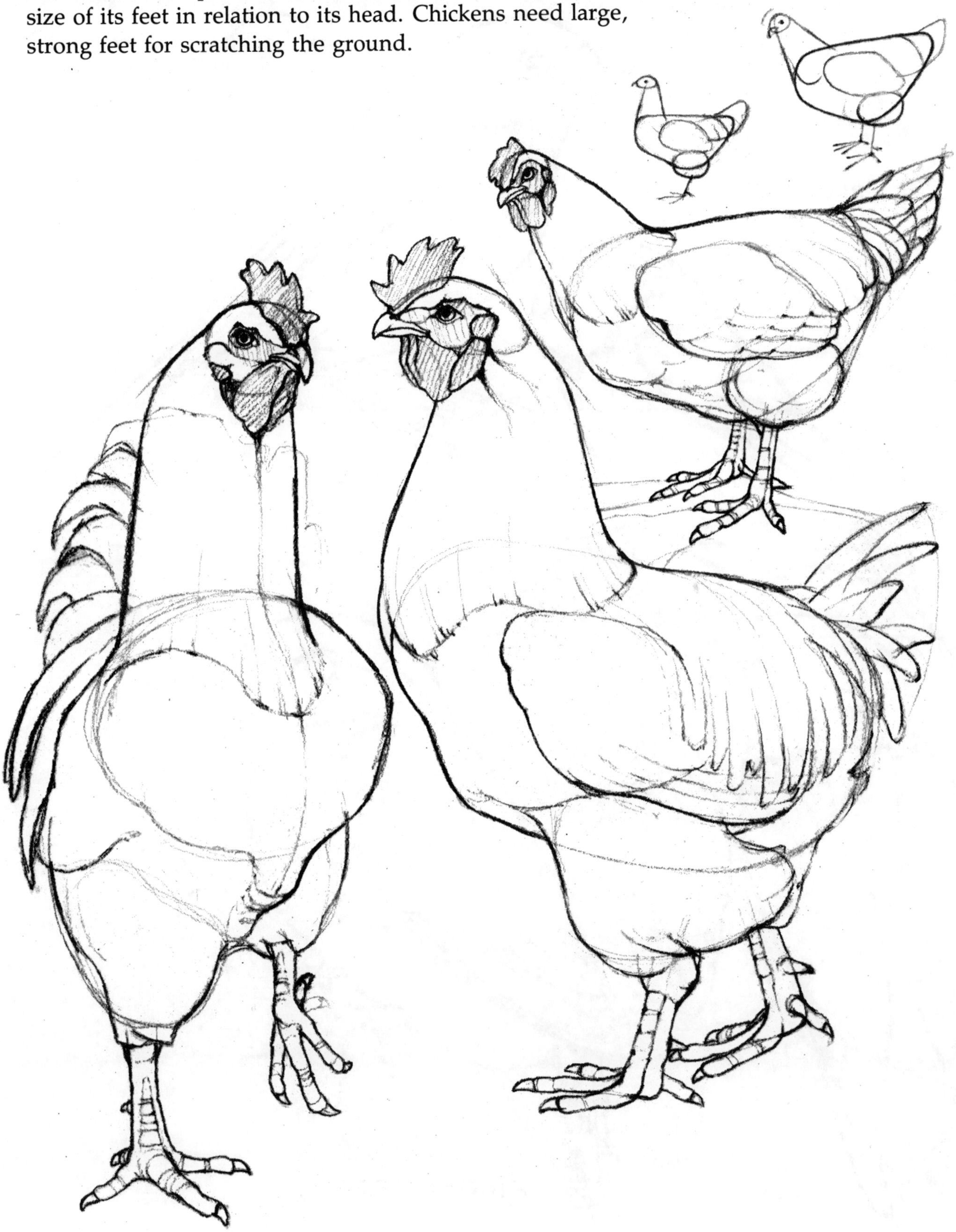

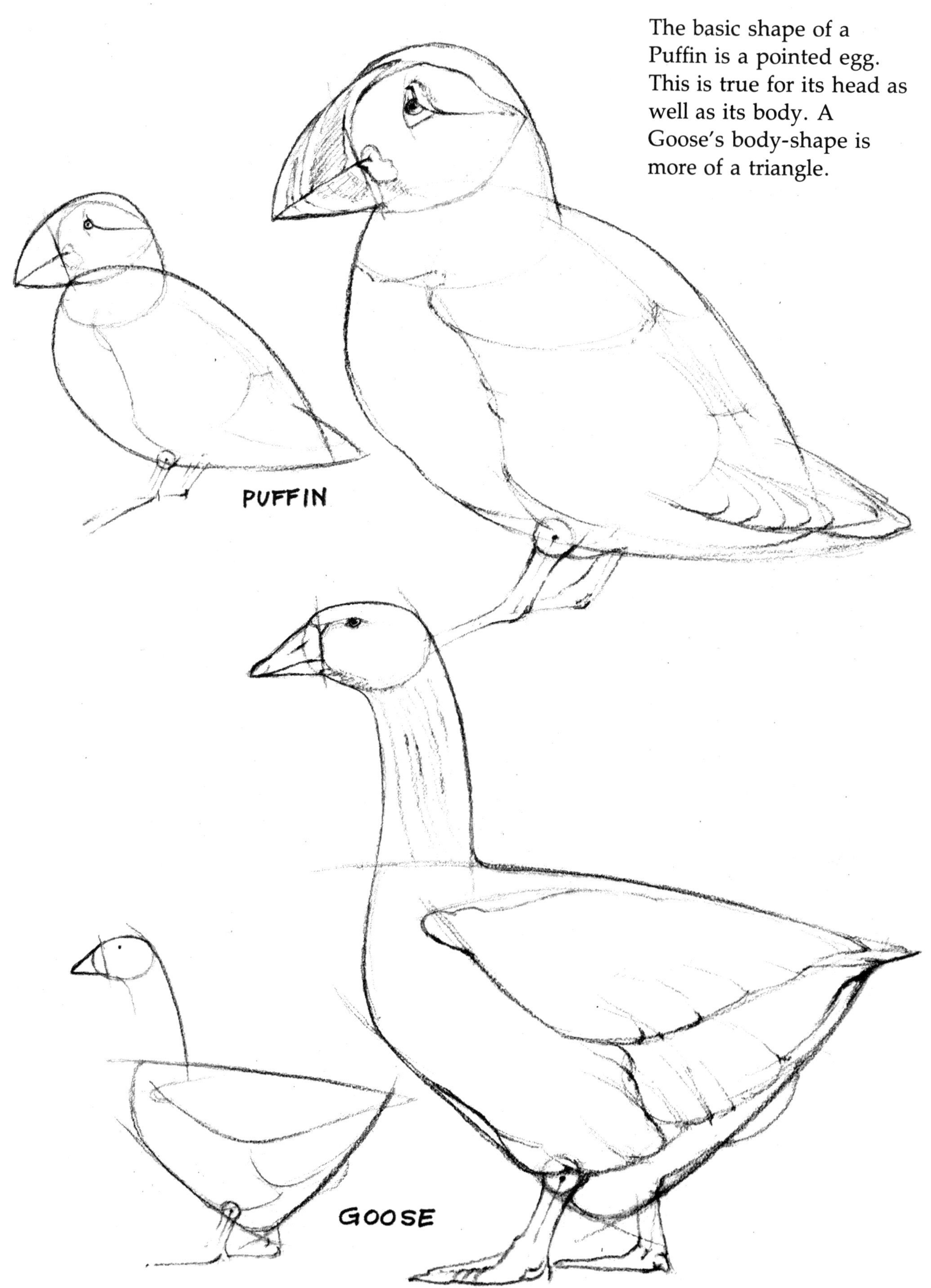

The basic shape of a Puffin is a pointed egg. This is true for its head as well as its body. A Goose's body-shape is more of a triangle.

If you draw one particular bird from several viewpoints, you will get to understand its anatomy more quickly than if you always draw the same view.

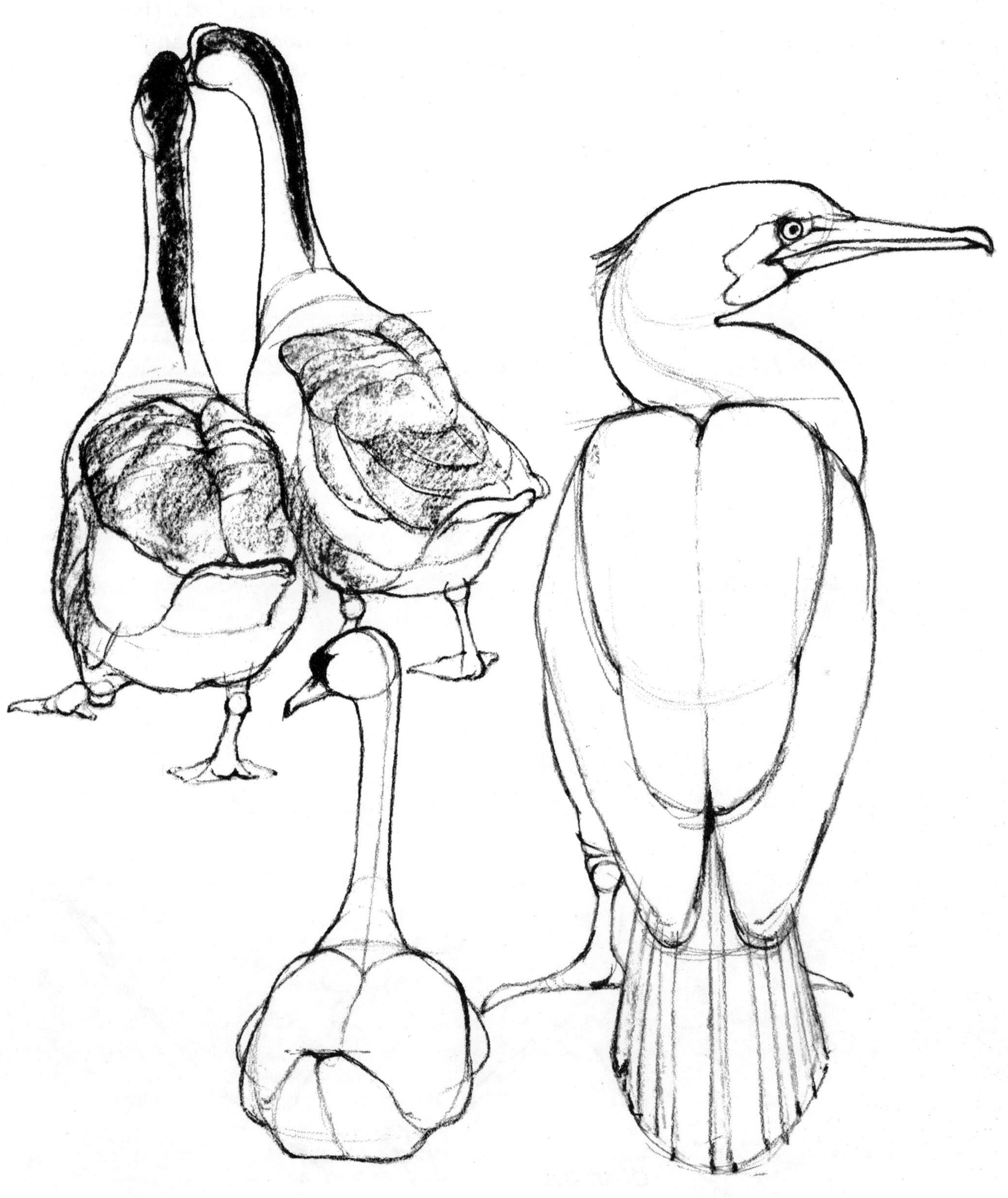

It is not easy to capture
movement when drawing
from photographs or
stuffed birds. I find it
helps to hold my pencil
vertically (making sure it
is at right angles to the
floor) and then run my
eyes down it noting the
position and angles of the
various parts of the
subject's body.

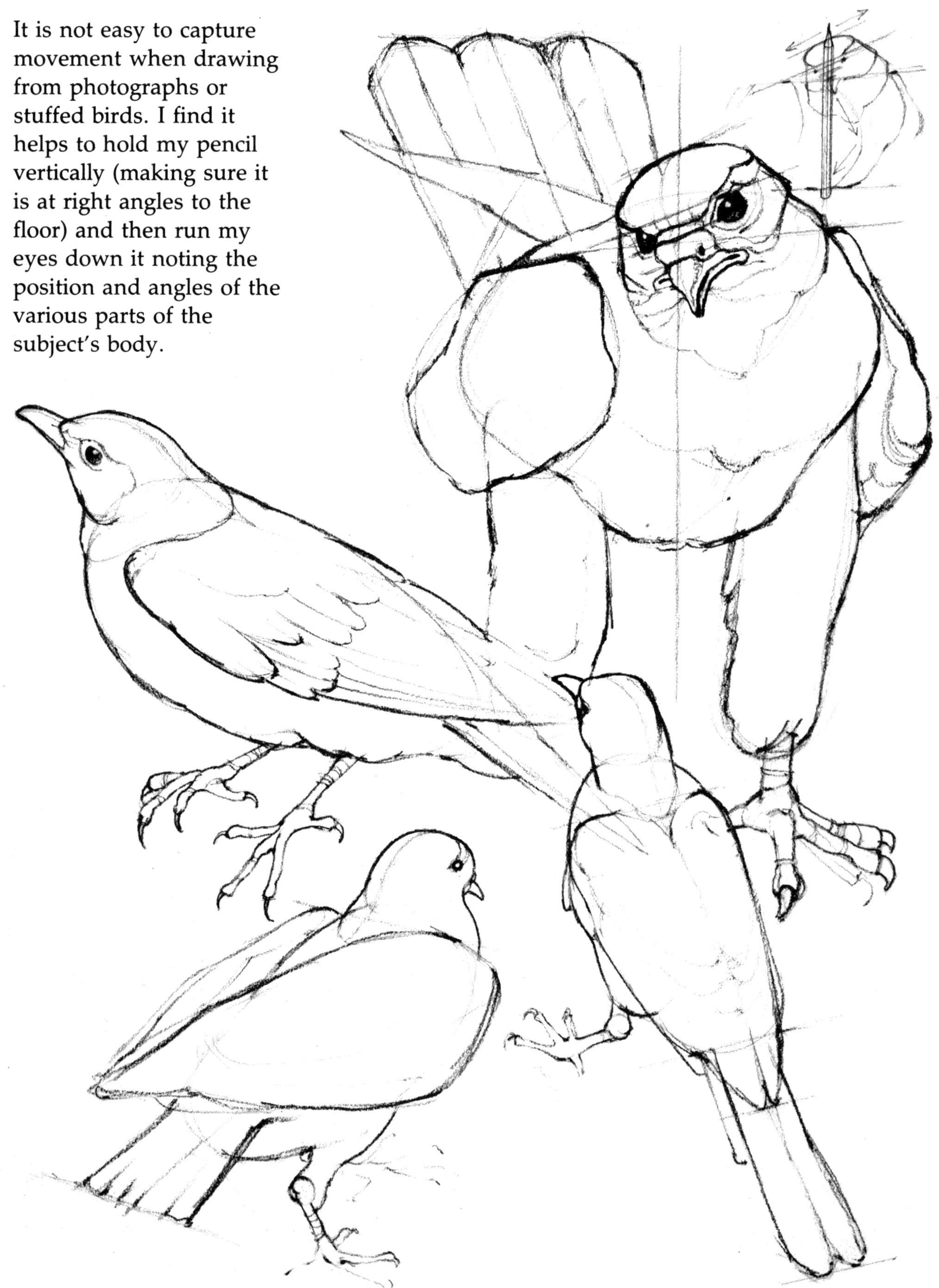

Step-by-step

The following pages show the development from first lines to the finished drawing. Draw the basic lines, and don't be timid about adding imaginary ones such as those marked 'A' to help you get the correct position of features in relation to one another. For instance, the lower vertical line on this page helps to establish correctly the curve of the neck in relation to the head. Remember, to get the proportions right, you must continually compare length, width and shape of the various areas (see pp. 14–16)

Note the direction from which light is coming and put in shaded areas. Vary line and shading by varying the pressure on your pencil. In the finished drawing opposite notice that the line is soft in light areas and heavy in dark ones.

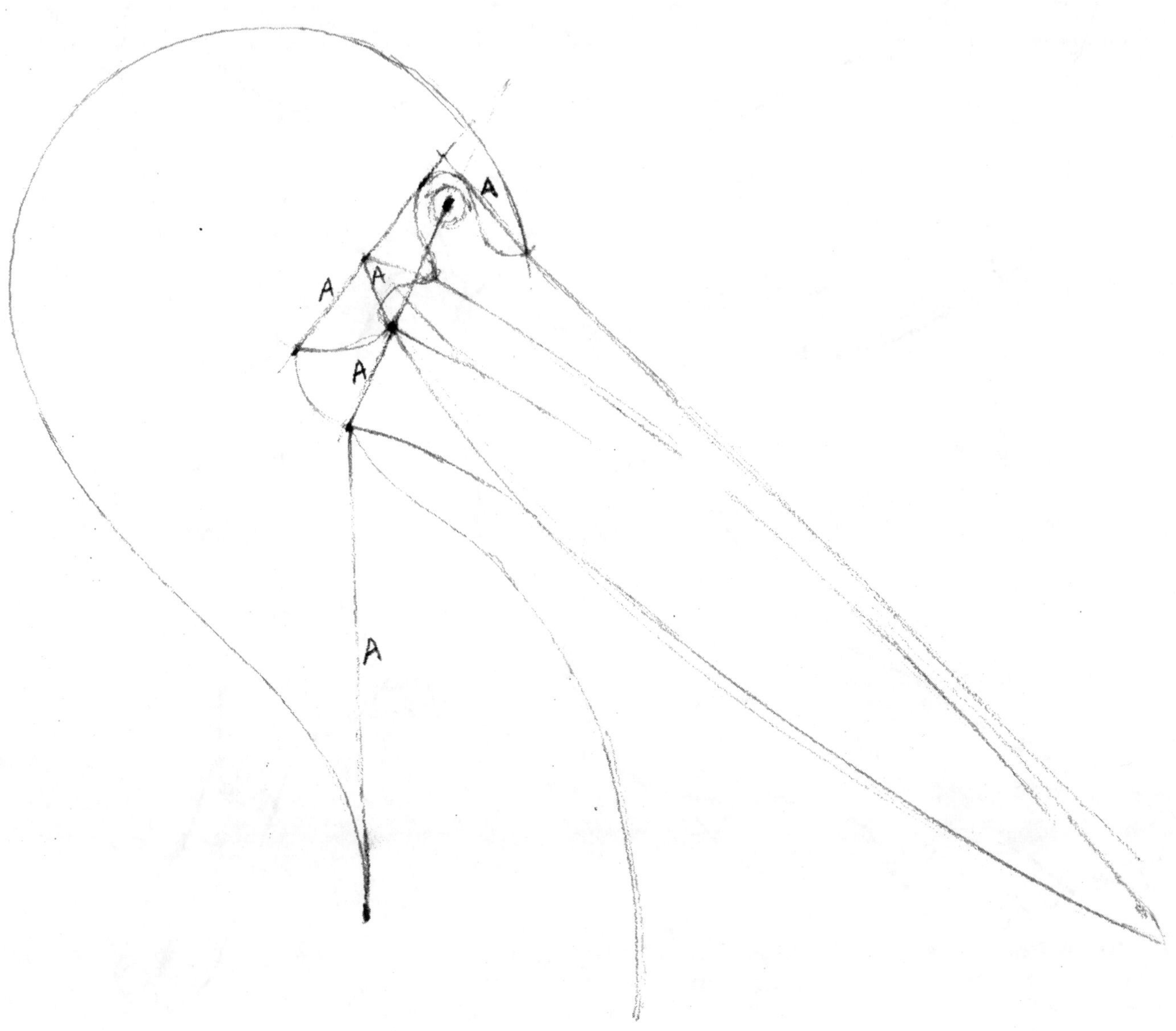

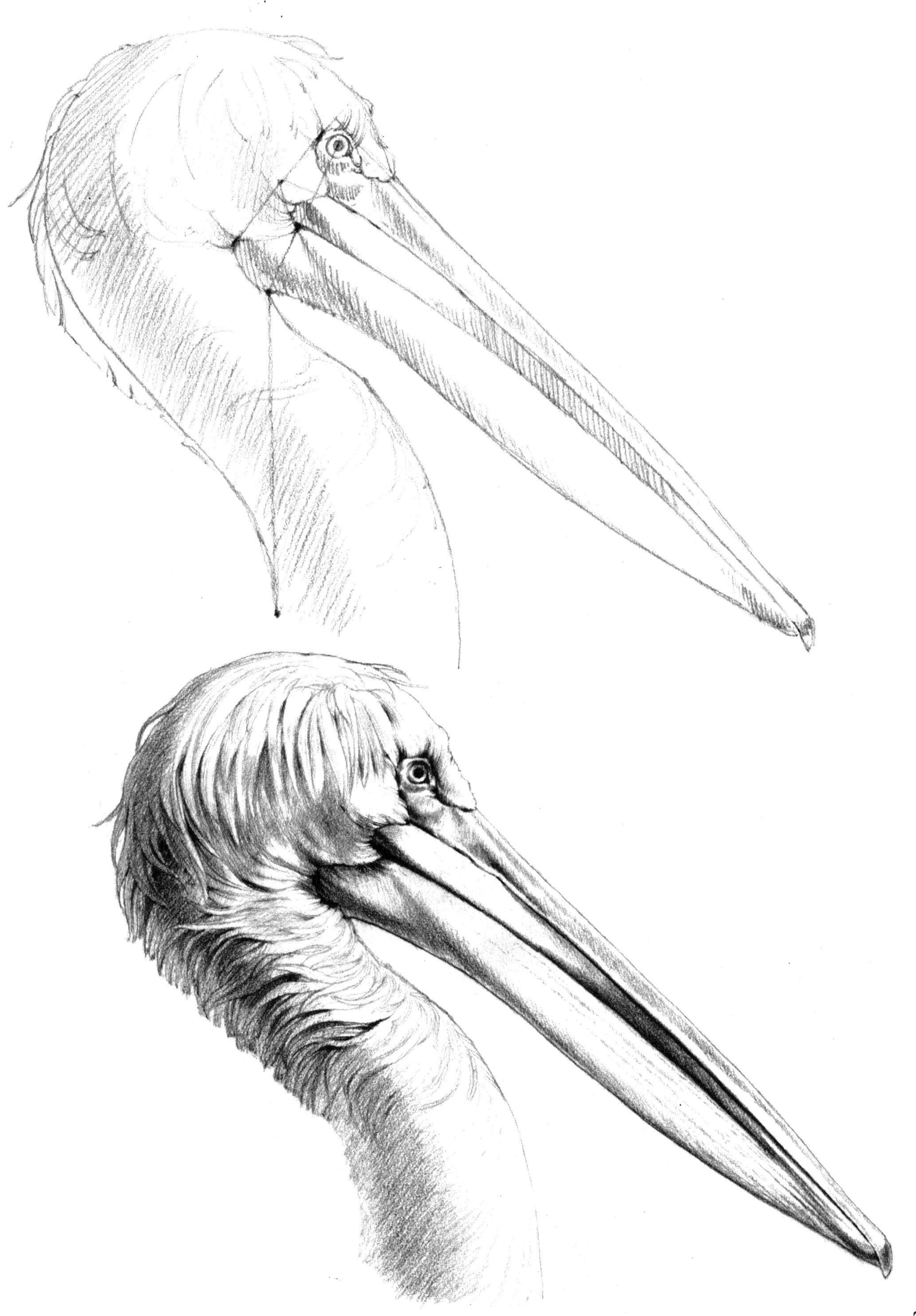

A Lapwing. If you half-close your eyes, most of the detail will
be shut out which helps you to see your subject in its simplest
form.

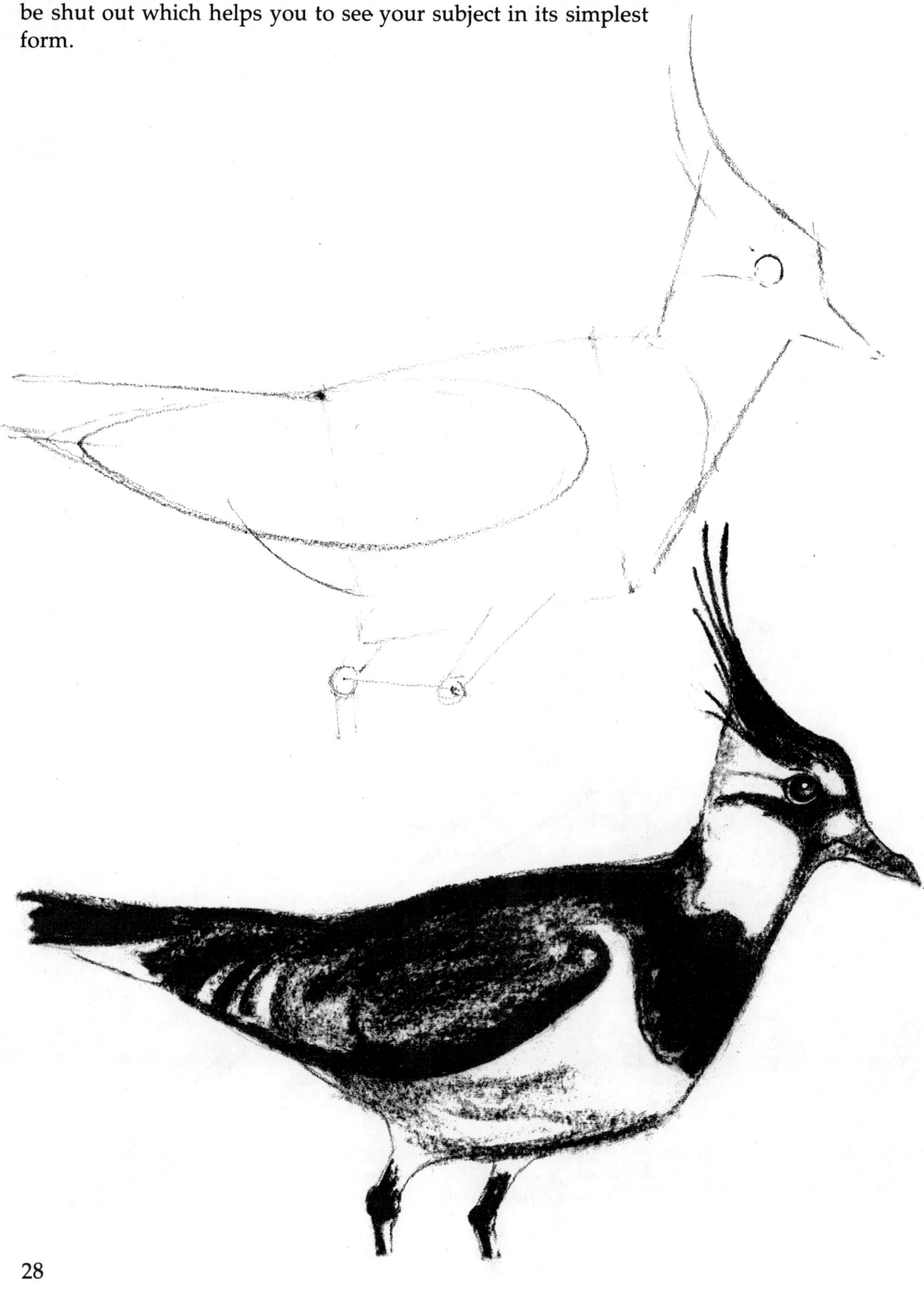

28

This pen and ink drawing of a Little Owl was finished with a wash of diluted ink.

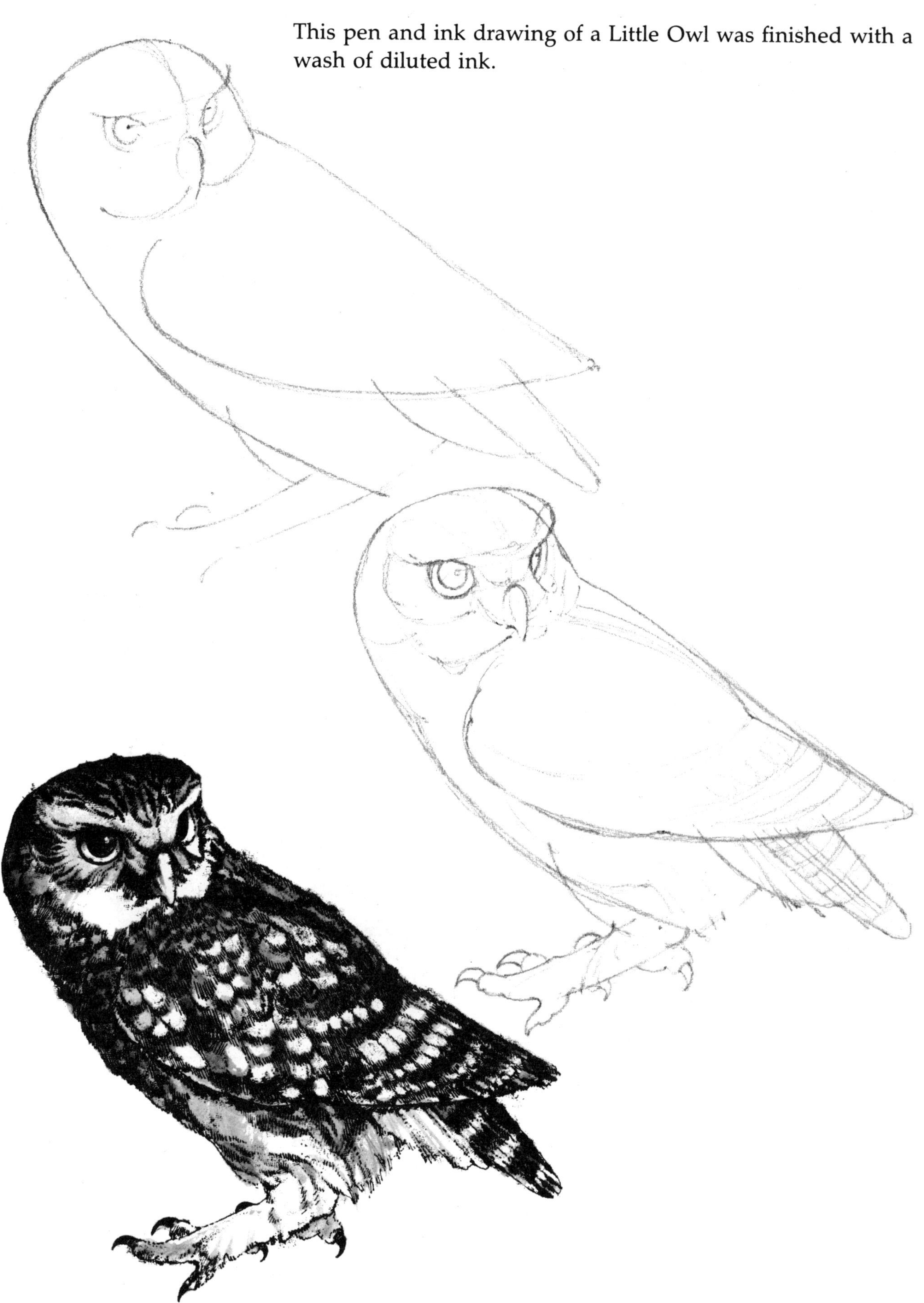

The basic drawing of this
Crowned Crane was done
in a soft pencil (2B). The
details were put in with a
fibre pen (in this case a
fine Pentel) then lightly
brushed with clean water.
It is a technique that
needs practice, but it can
produce pleasant results.

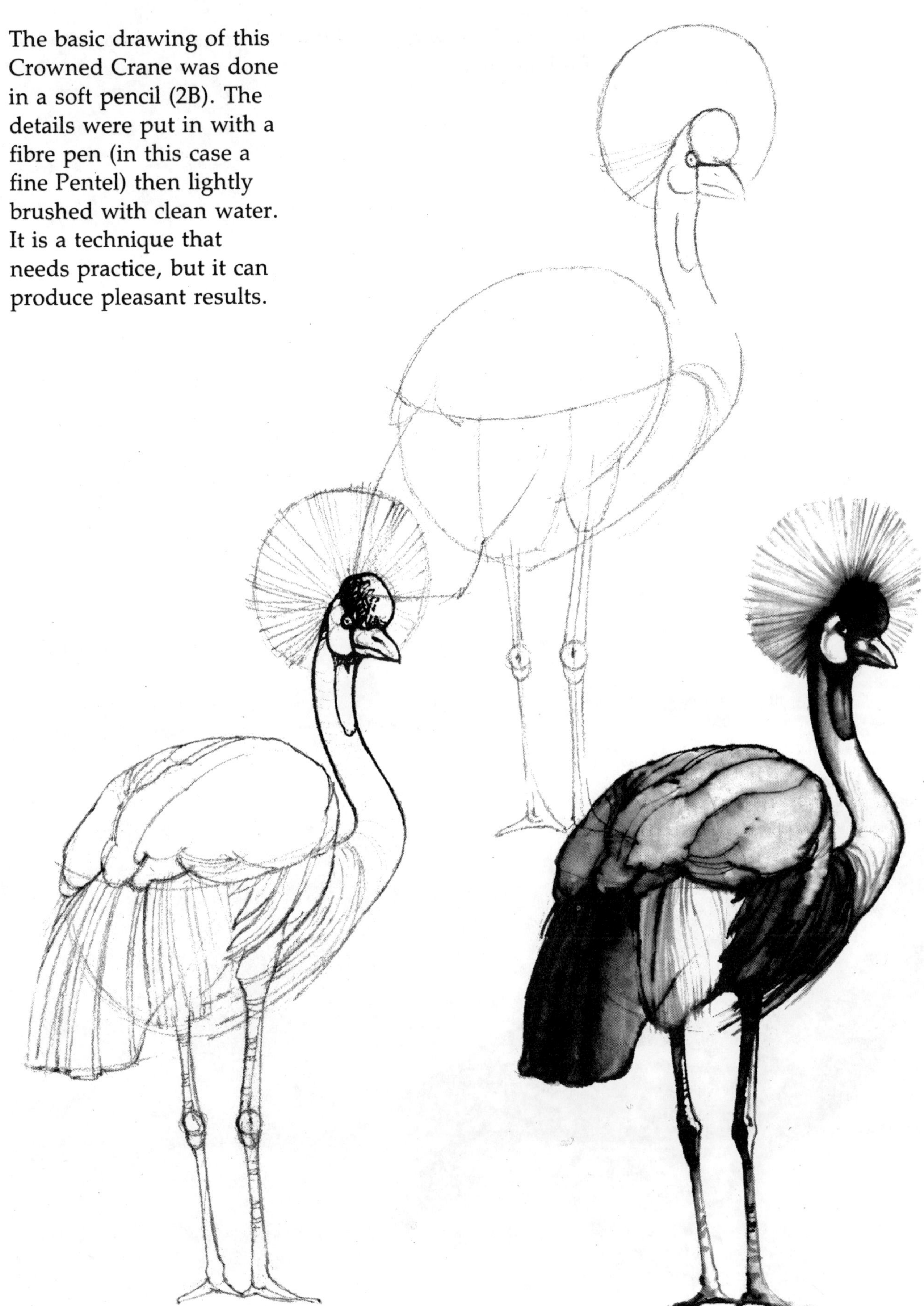

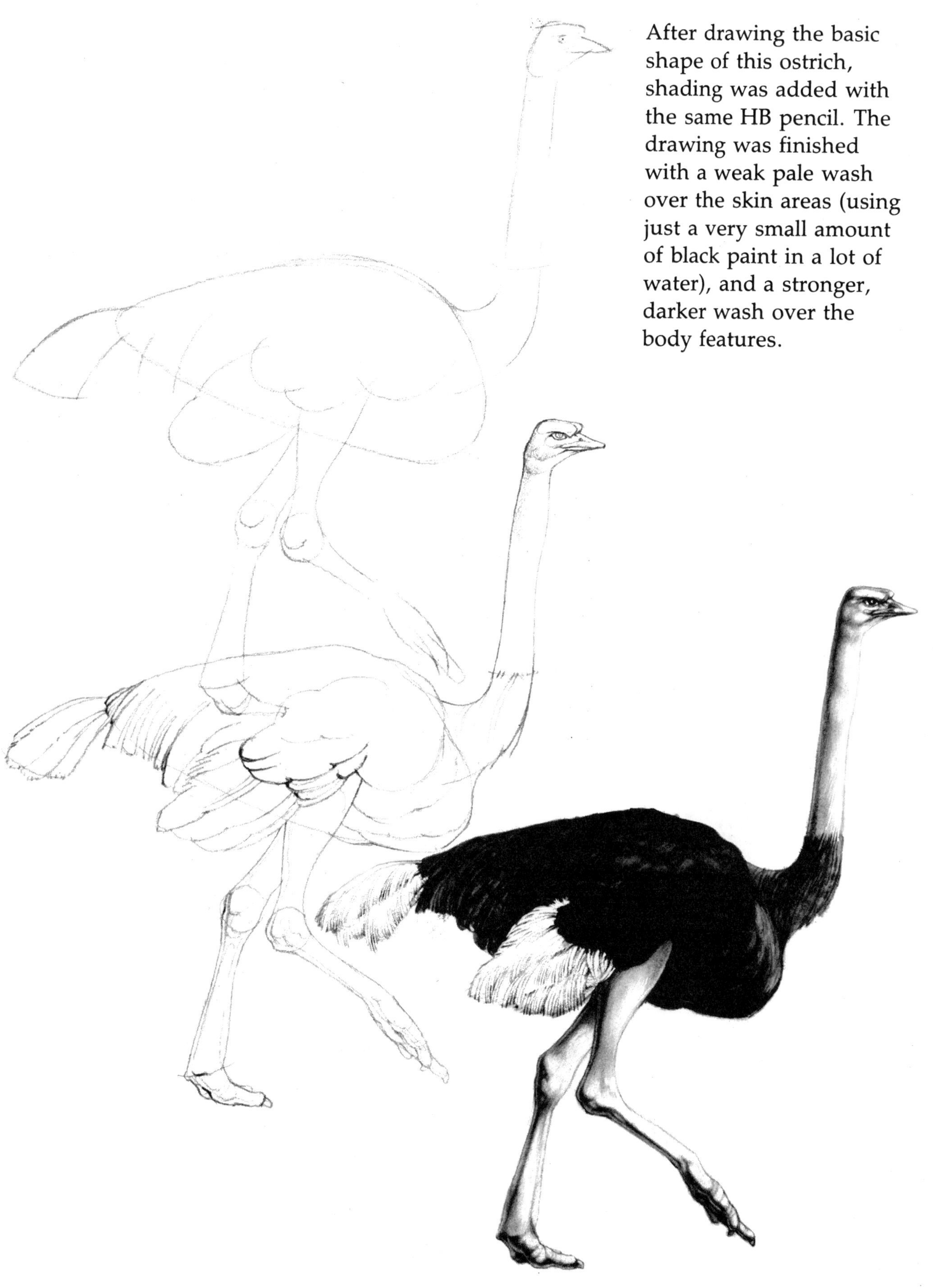

After drawing the basic shape of this ostrich, shading was added with the same HB pencil. The drawing was finished with a weak pale wash over the skin areas (using just a very small amount of black paint in a lot of water), and a stronger, darker wash over the body features.

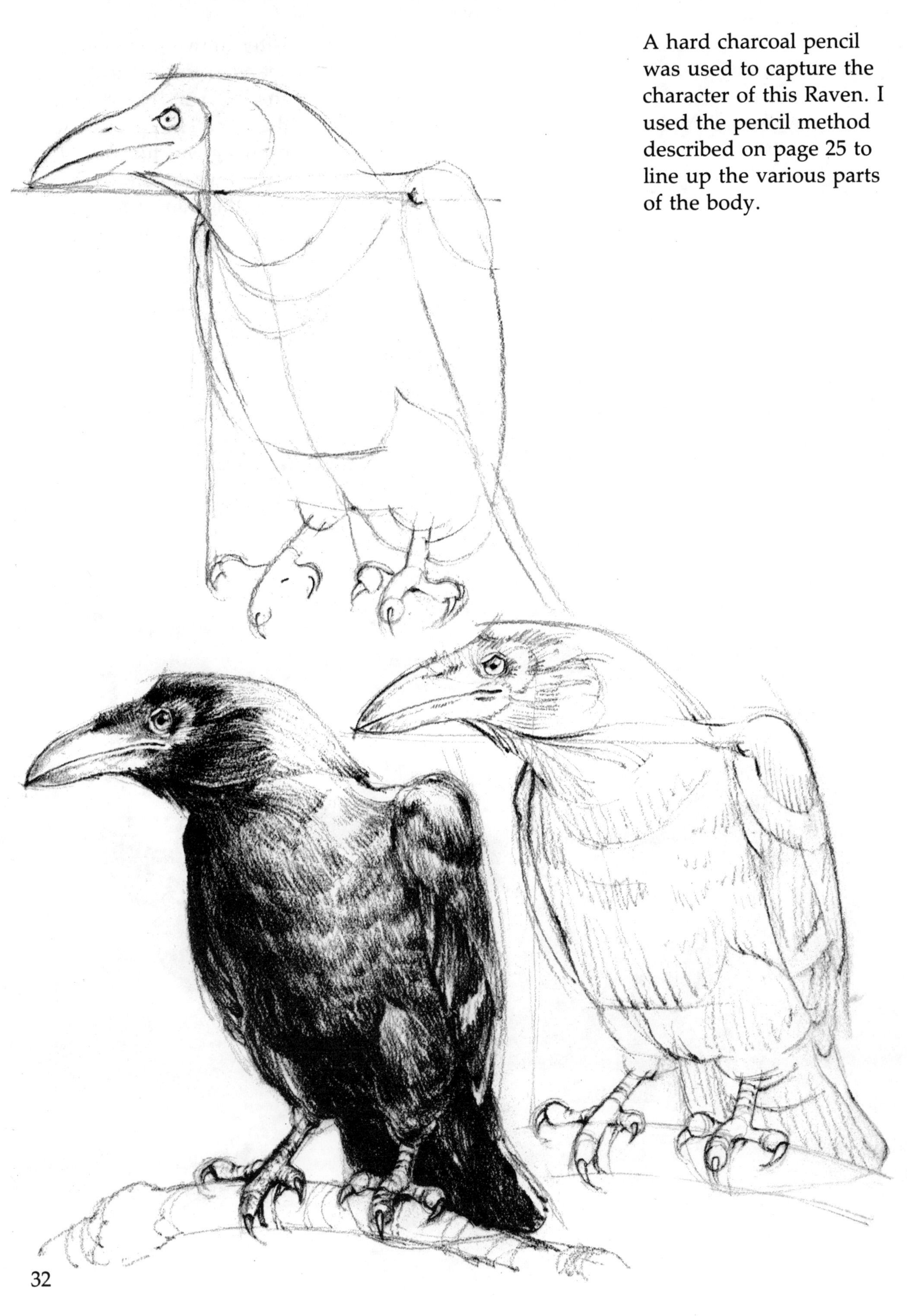

A hard charcoal pencil
was used to capture the
character of this Raven. I
used the pencil method
described on page 25 to
line up the various parts
of the body.

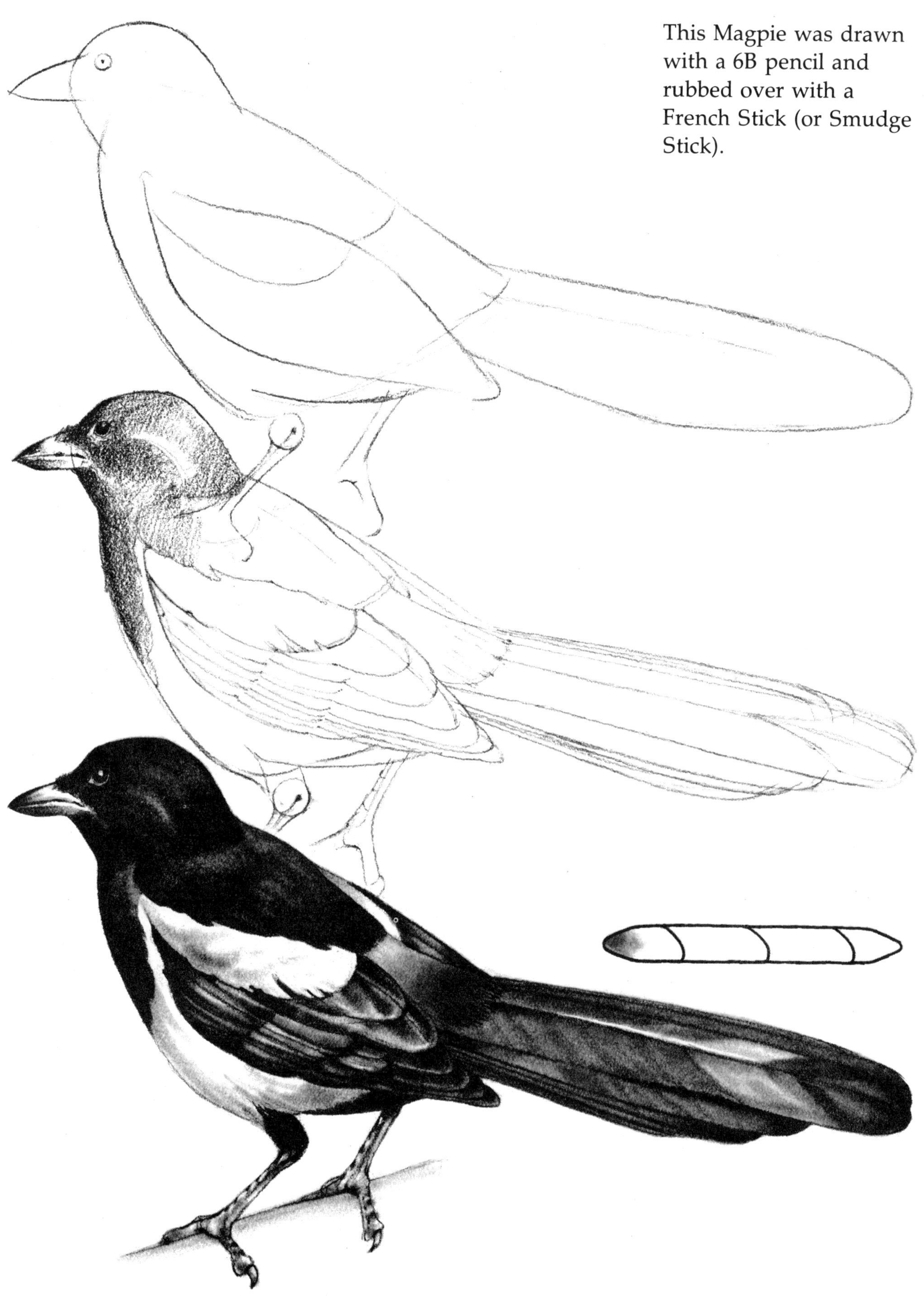

This Magpie was drawn with a 6B pencil and rubbed over with a French Stick (or Smudge Stick).

Composition

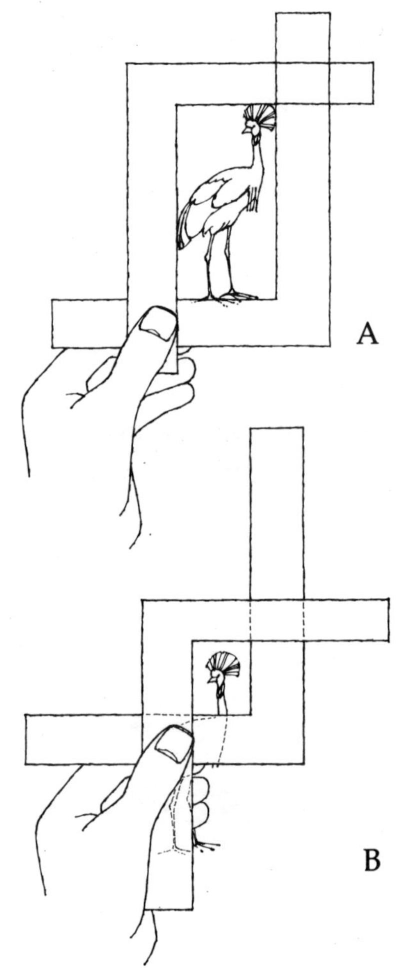

This does not only apply to large, finished paintings. Deciding where to place even the smallest sketch or doodle on a scribbling pad involves composition. Your drawing will be greatly affected by its position on the paper.

When you are drawing more than one bird on a sheet of paper, the placing of each one is important. Try as many variations as possible.

Before you begin a drawing, think about how you will place it on the paper—even a few seconds' thought may save you having to start your drawing again. One of the most common mistakes is to start by putting the head in the centre of the paper, regardless of which way the body goes. Never distort your drawing in order to get it all in, or you will wonder why it looks wrong.

Cut out two pieces of card so that they form corners. Hold them up between you and your subject. Position them so that the inside edges touch the furthest points of the bird (A). This will show you the correct proportion of the area taken up by its body, and will help you to position your drawing on the paper.

Another way to help you compose your drawing is to form the corners into a picture frame (B).

The alternative is to use a large sheet of paper so that you can leave plenty of space around your drawing. The paper can then be trimmed down to produce a pleasing composition.

Before starting an elaborate drawing, do a few very rough sketches of the main shapes to help you decide on the final composition. When you have decided which to use, rule a faint network of lines—diagonal, vertical and horizontal—over this preliminary sketch and on the piece of paper to be used for the finished drawing. (Take care that both pieces are the same proportion.) You will then have a number of reference points to enable you to transfer the composition to the final drawing.

Action

When you first attempt to draw birds in action, choose the more simple and continuous actions, such as cleaning, eating and drinking.

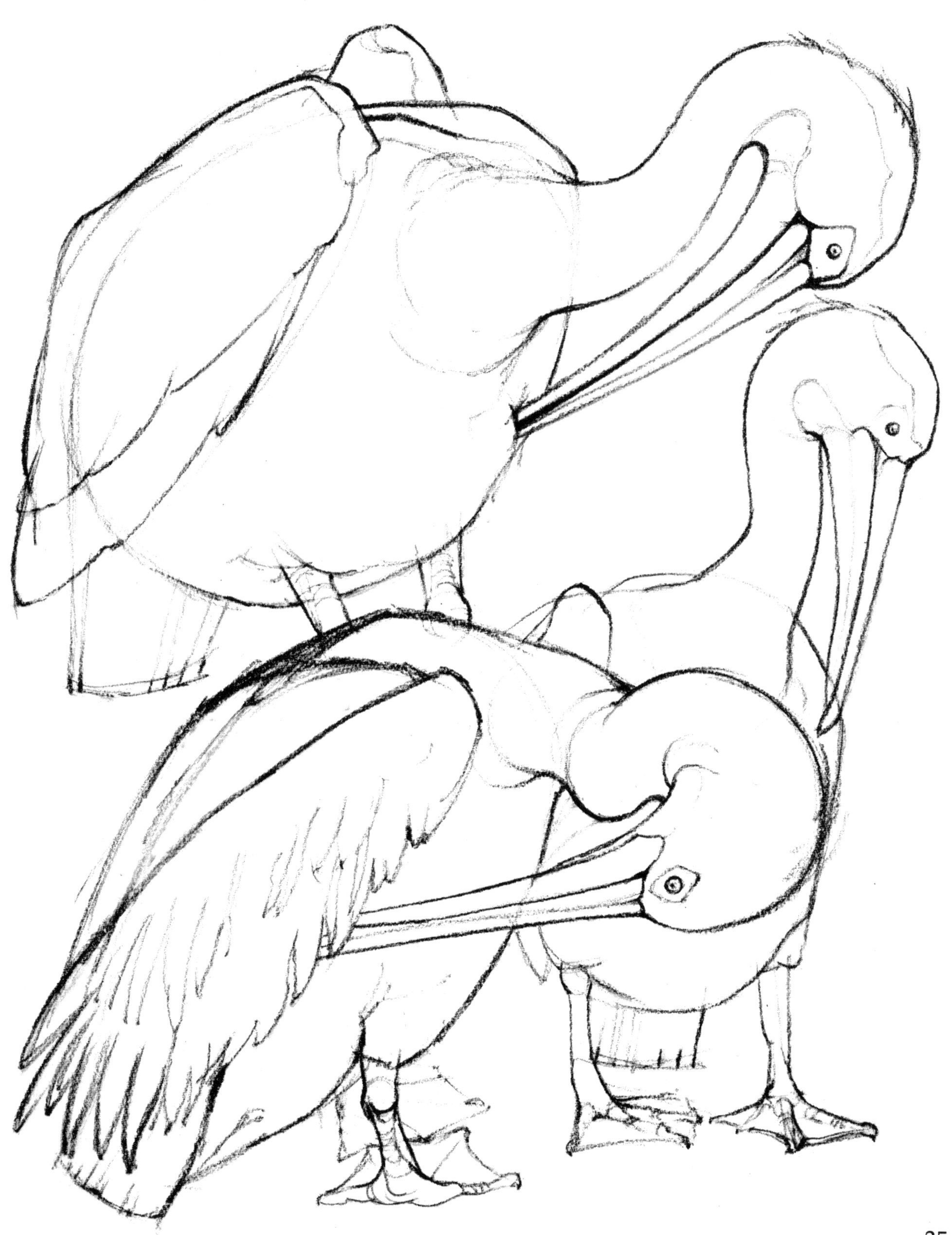

Draw quickly, ignoring details. Concentrate on capturing the
basic shape (as in the small drawings here), and the
movement in the pose. Facial and other details can be put in
later.

Drawing live birds in flight is extremely difficult; but if you
work from photographs (as you really must) make sure they
are of good quality. Notice the wing and body movements of
the various birds here.

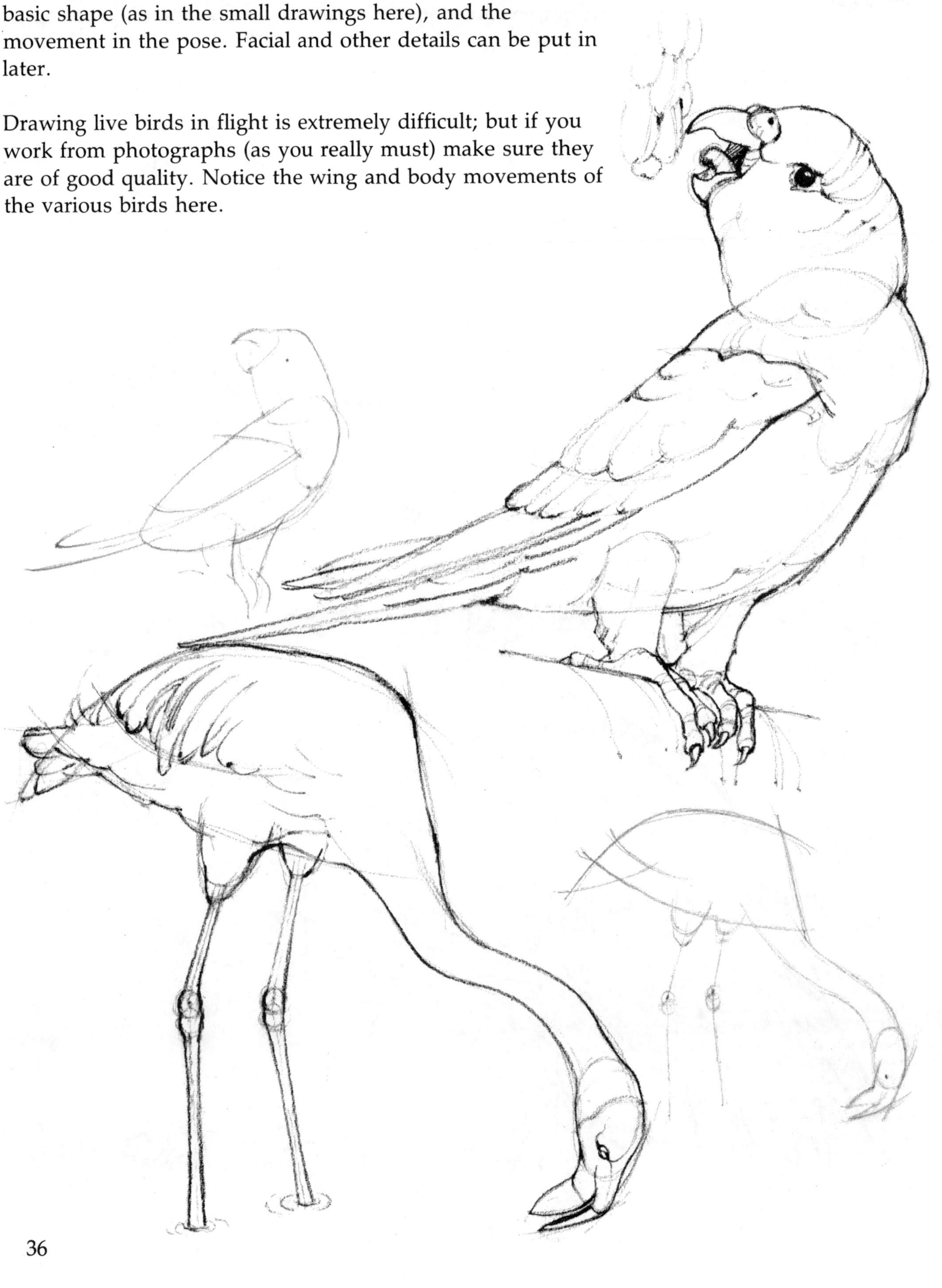

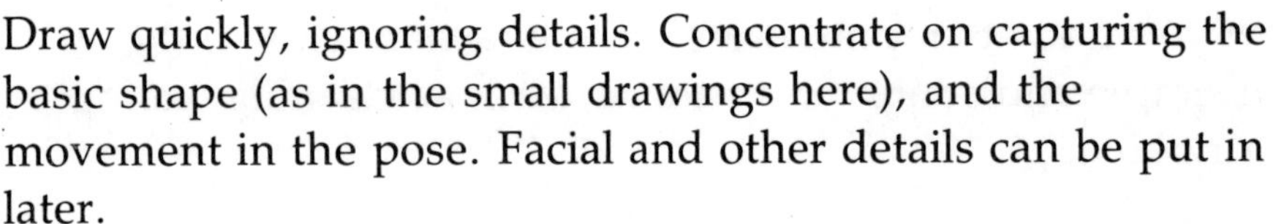

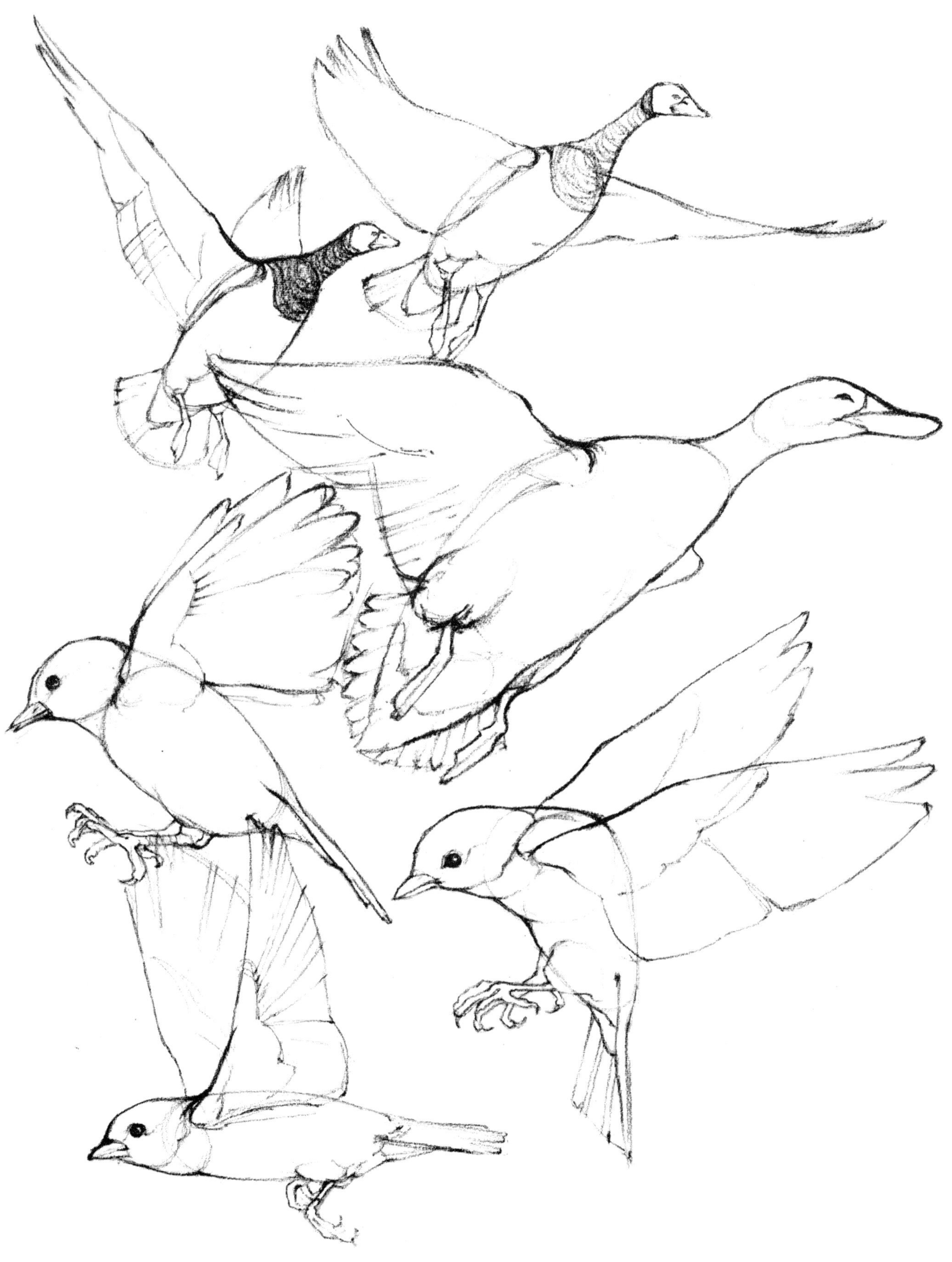

Be careful not to copy the two-dimensional image of a
photograph; make yourself see the bird as living and
three-dimensional. Construct your drawing.

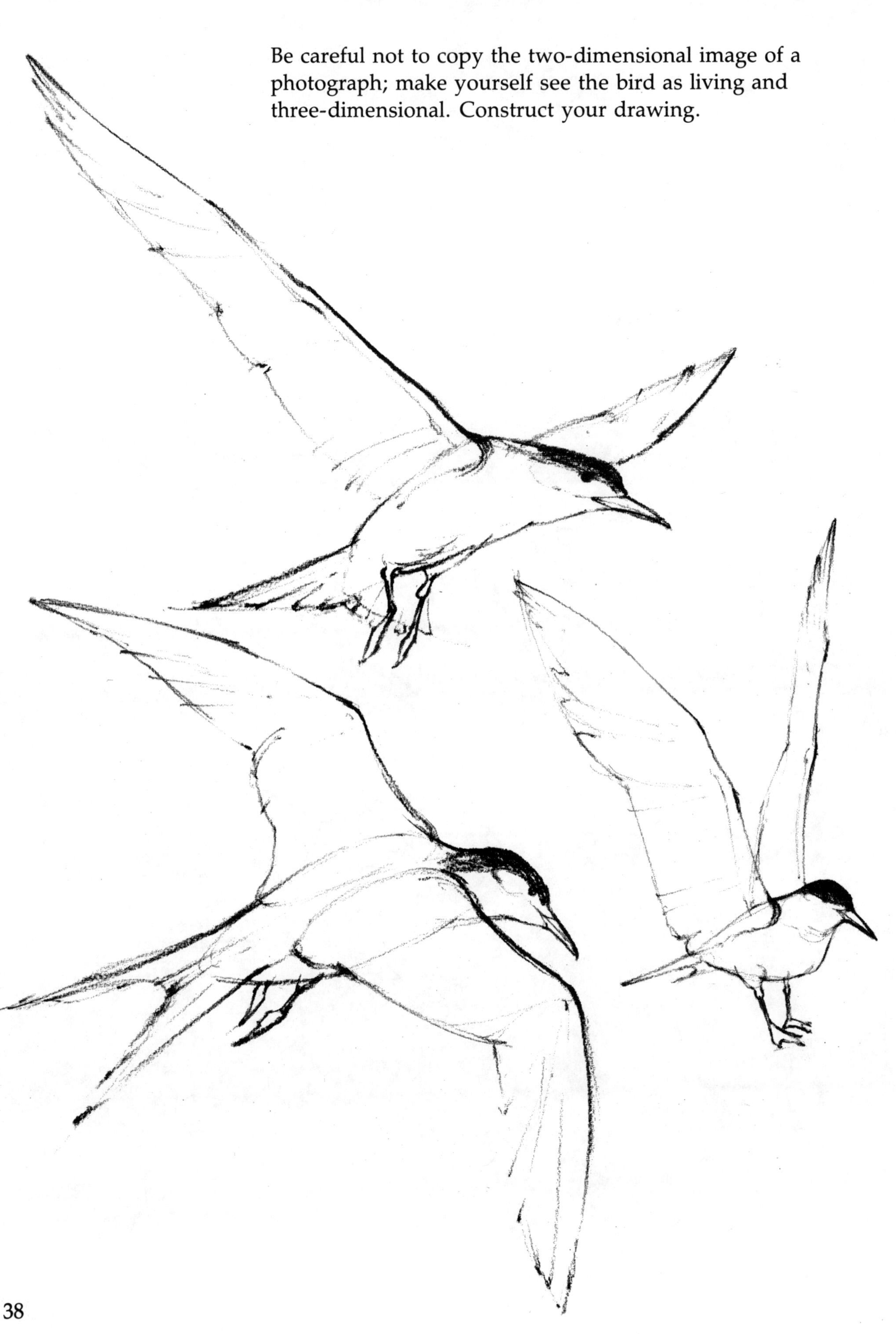

Notice how the head and wings fit into the body. Once again, draw quickly to produce lines full of movement.

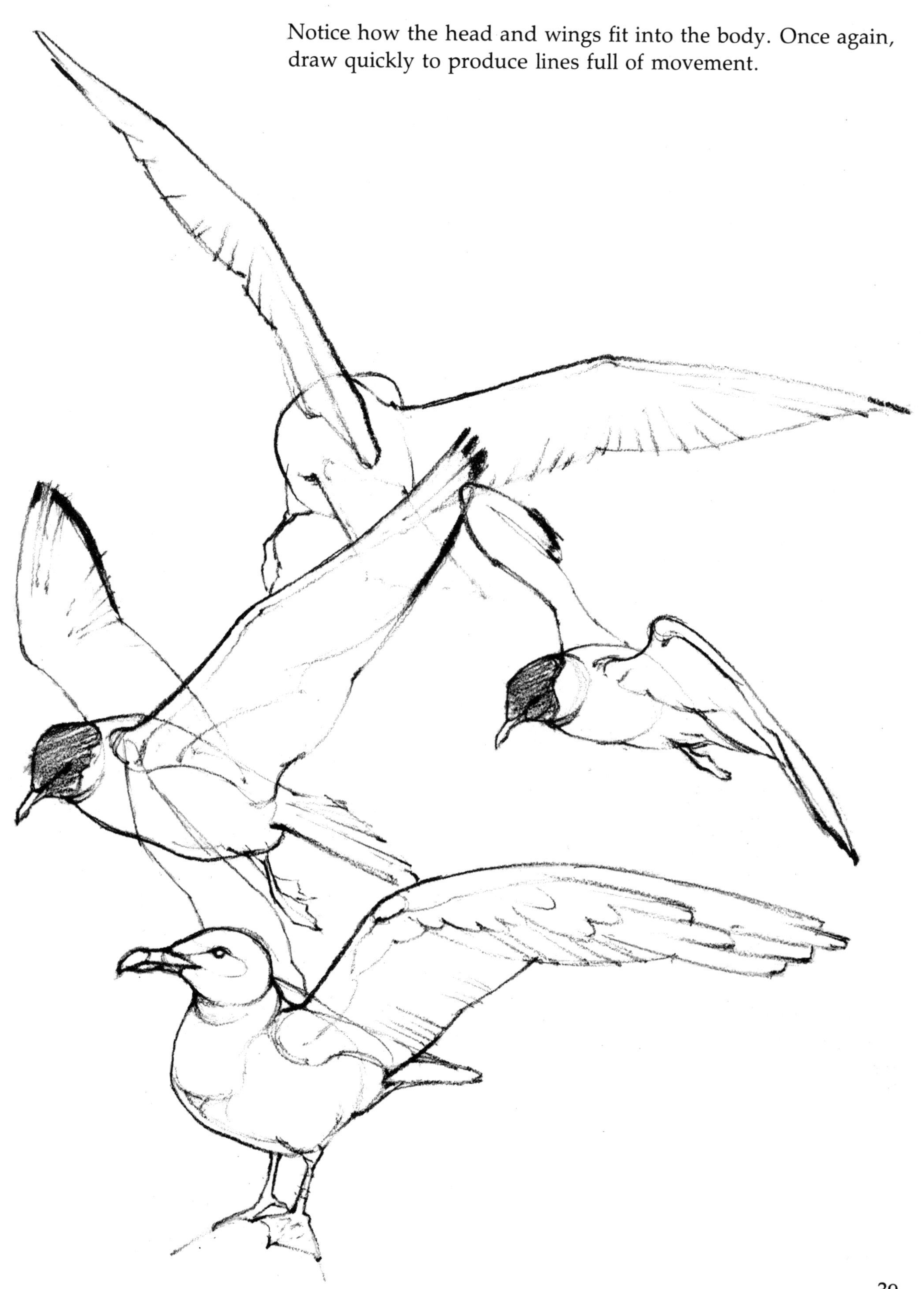

Tricks and techniques

This Skylark was drawn with a fibre pen. I then used a candle for the light areas. Finally, I washed over the whole drawing (except the stomach area) with watered-down black paint. You can increase the darkness of a wash by mixing in more paint; use a watercolour board.

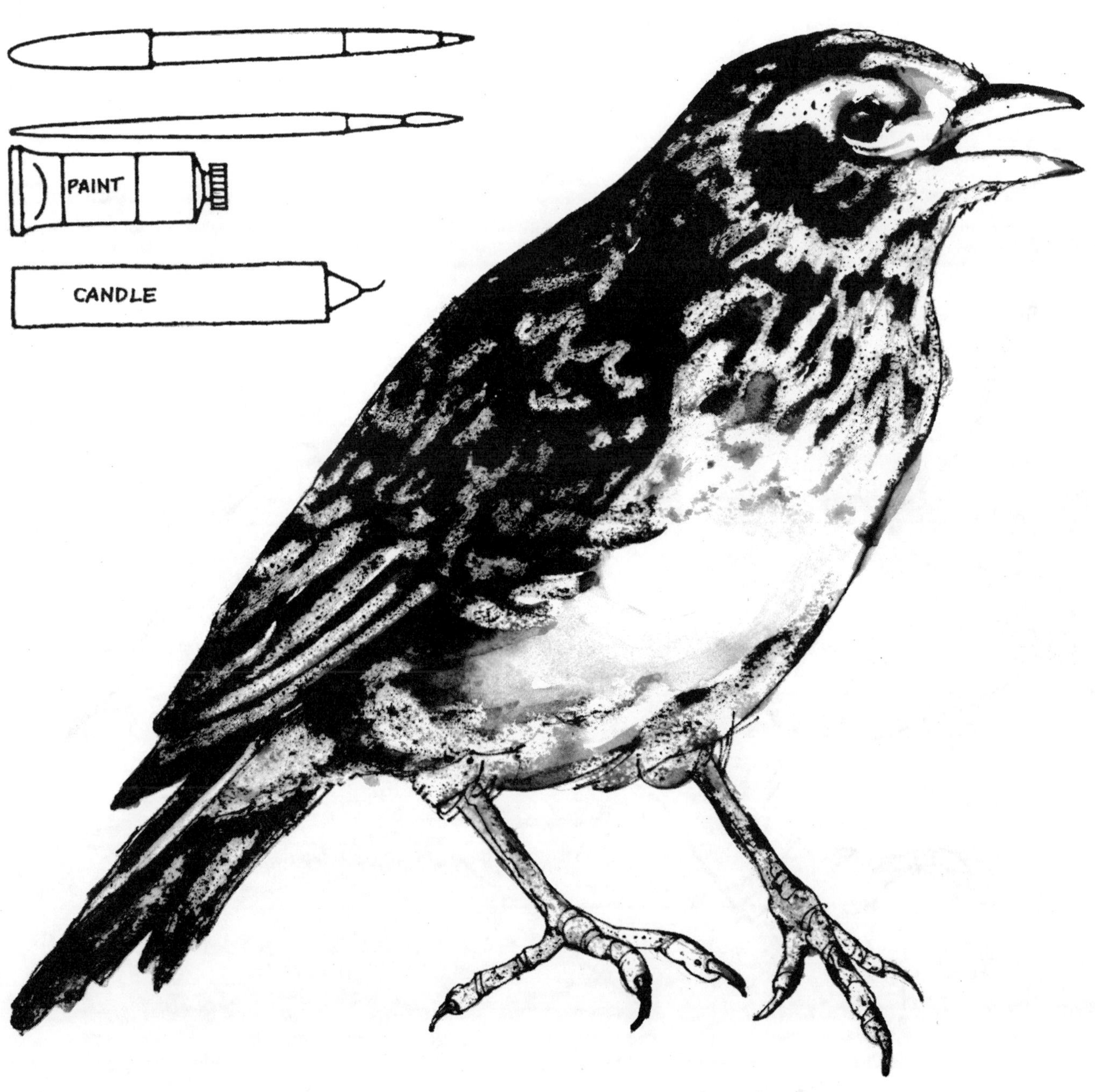

The Great Tit was drawn with pen and ink and dabbed with a finger when still wet. The Thrush was drawn with a fibre pen and then some parts were lightly washed over with clean water. I used a rough cartridge paper.

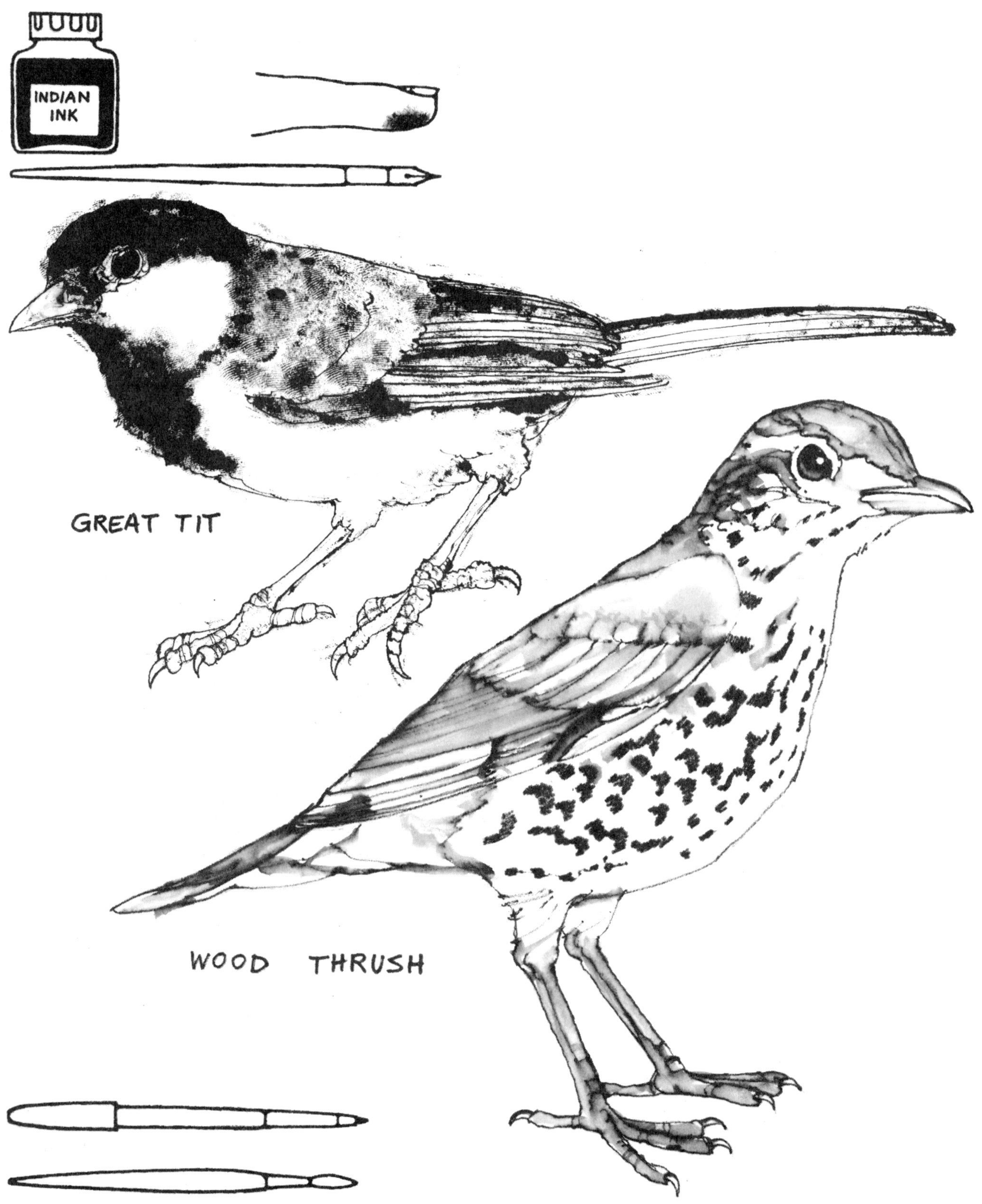

The Pheasant here was first drawn in pencil. I then painted
masking fluid on all the areas that were to remain white, and
when this was dry painted the whole area with Indian ink (I
have left most of the tail in that stage). Finally, when the ink
was dry, I used an eraser to remove the masking fluid. I drew
the Plover in the same way, except that I used a stipple brush
and paint instead of Indian ink, which made it possible to
vary the density of the dark areas. The drawings were made
on a rough-surfaced board.

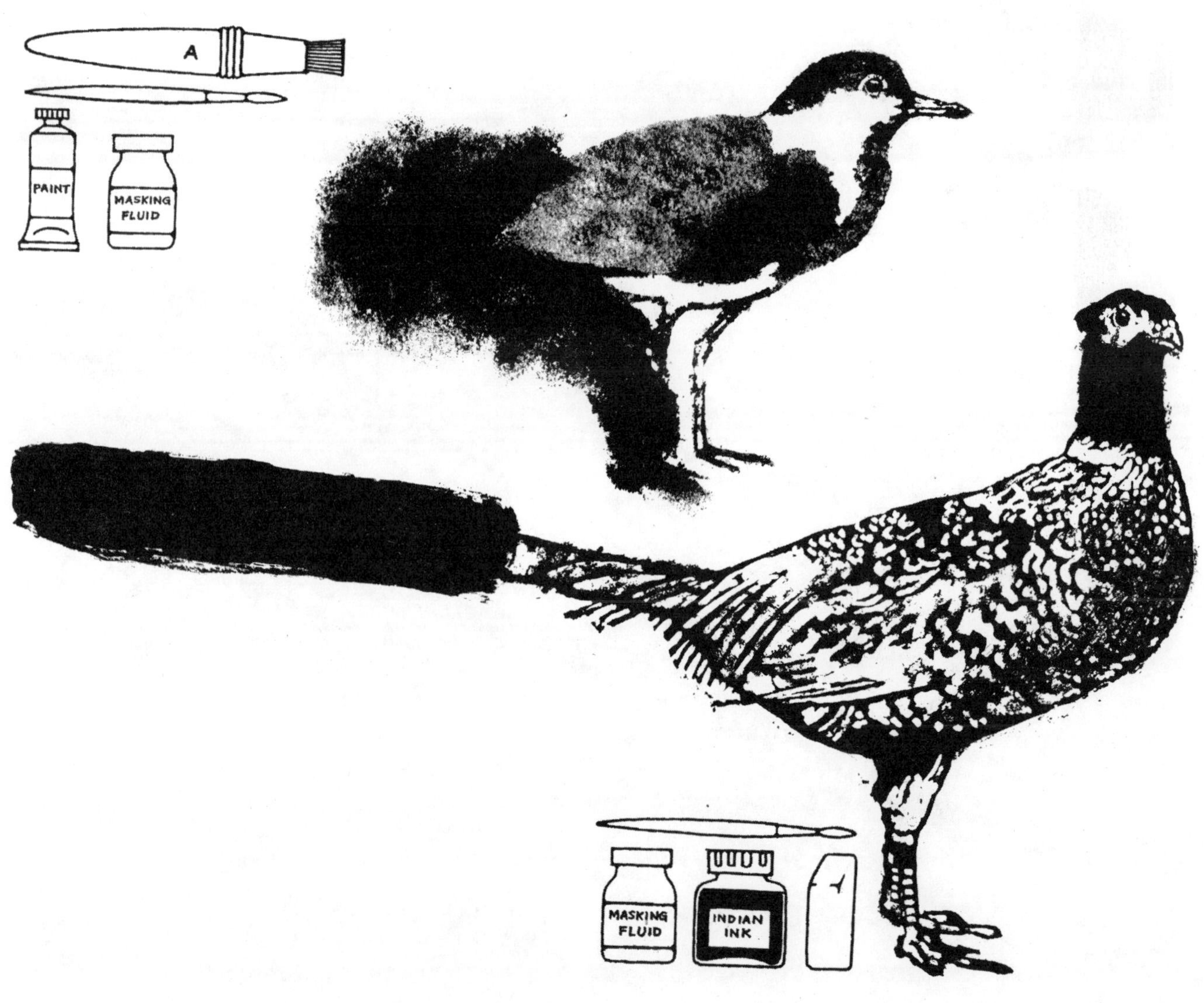

This Macaw was drawn with a wax crayon on rough cartridge paper.

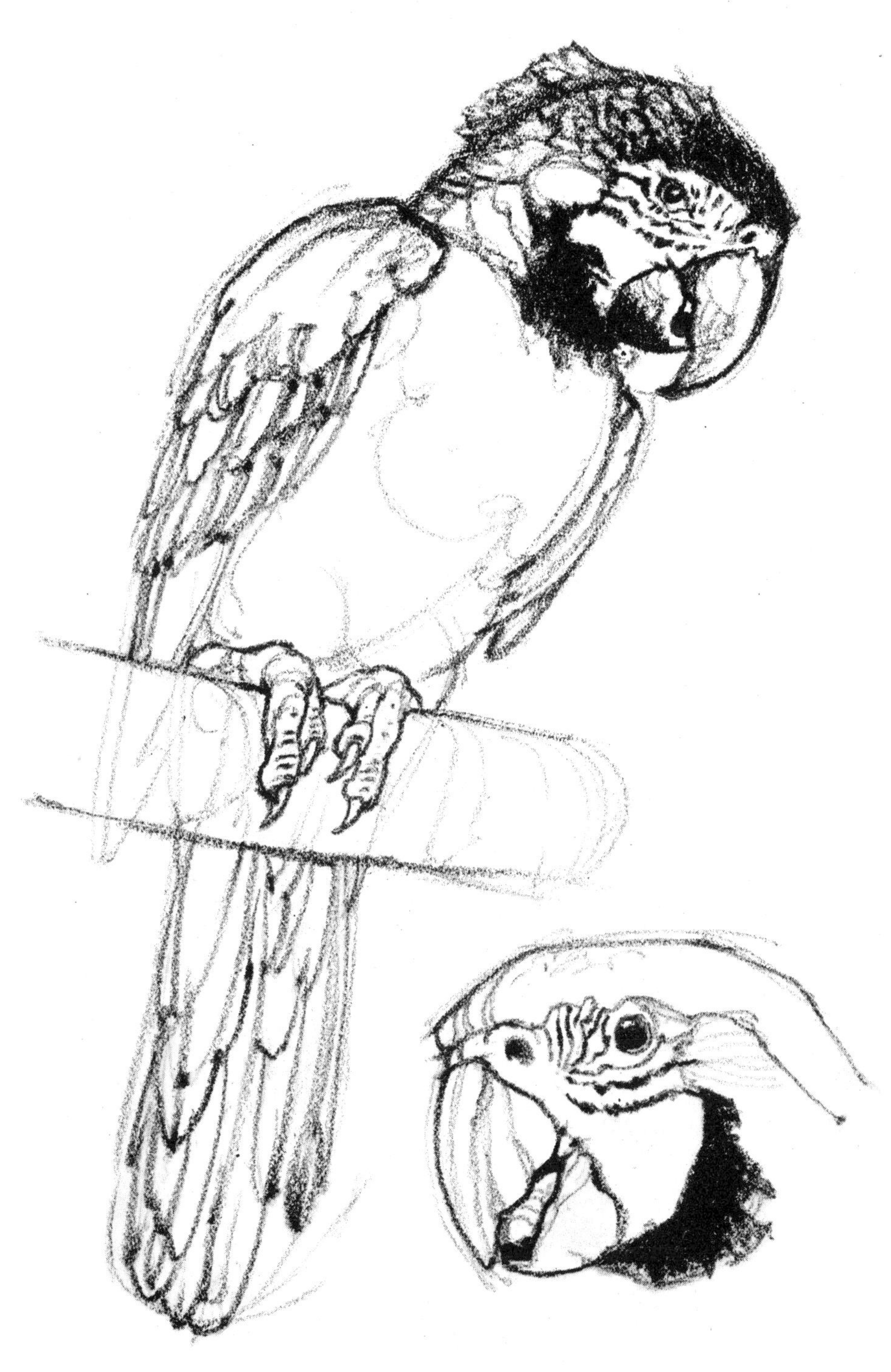

A Peruvian Penguin
drawn with a thick felt
pen. You cannot get
much detail or subtle line
with this medium.

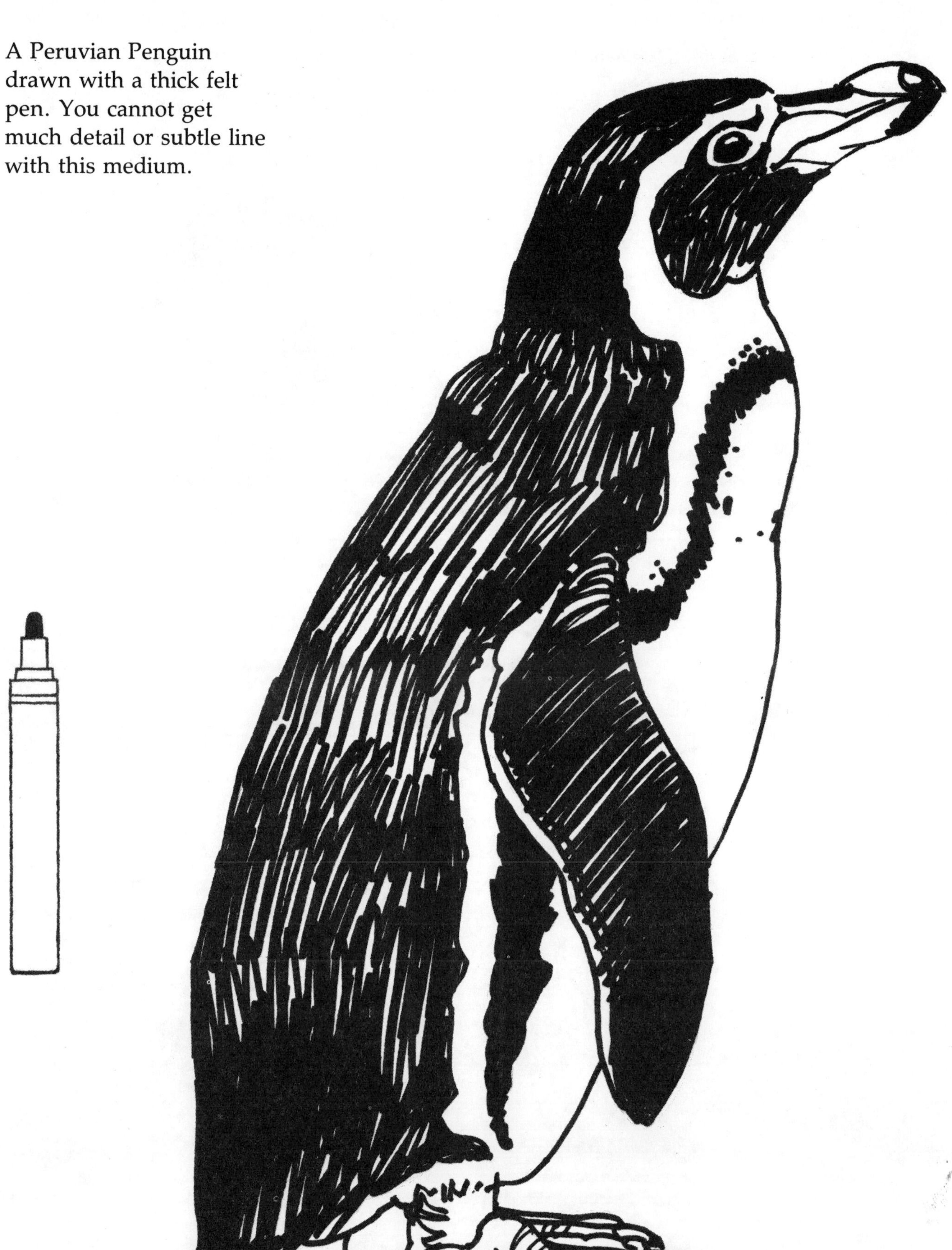

44

A brush and black paint
were used for this
Razorbill. Be subtle; vary
the density of the wash.
Try using watercolour
paint on a watercolour
board.

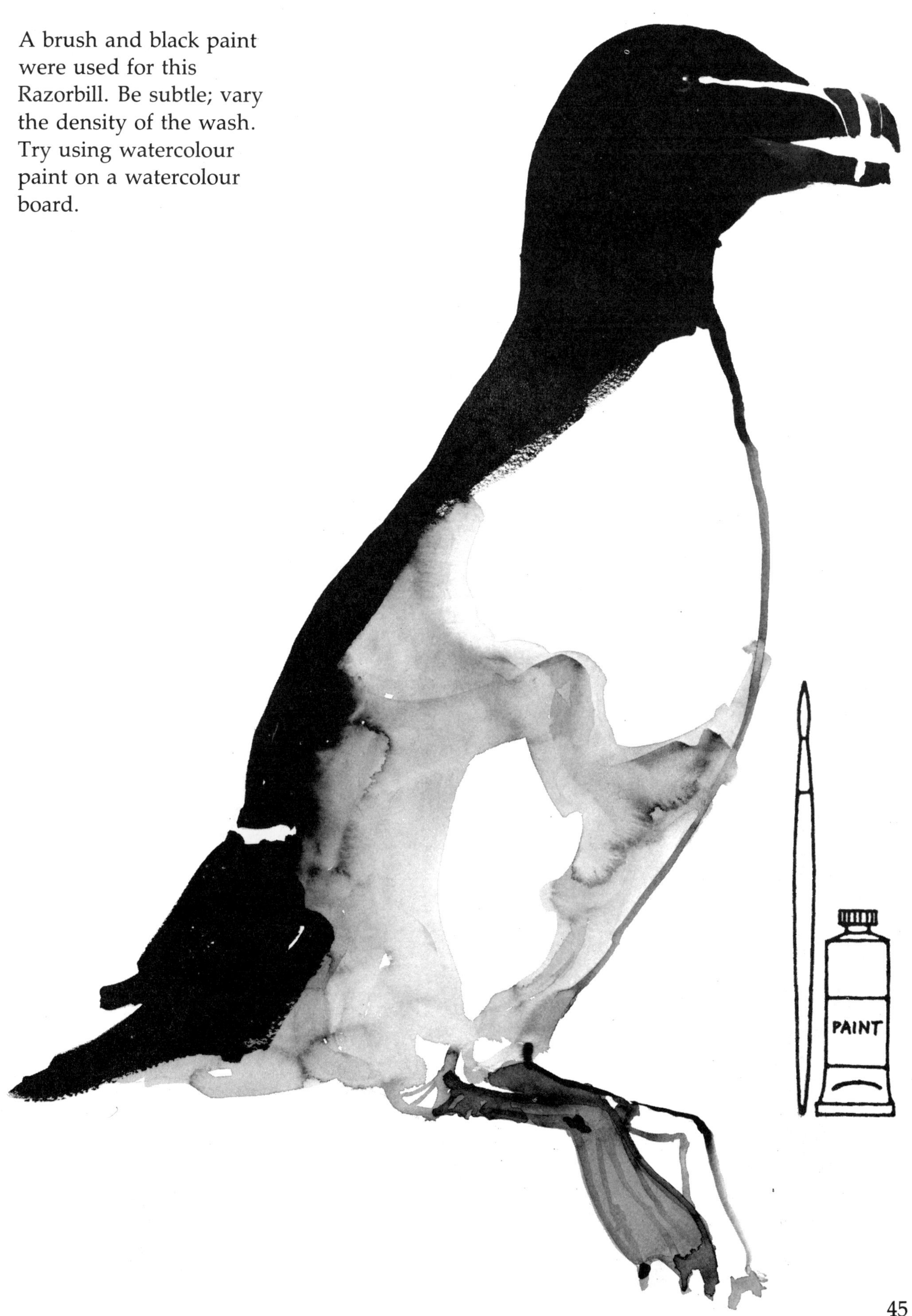

The magnificent Bald Eagle, emblem of the USA, was first drawn here with the *handle* of a brush dipped in ink and ther painted with the brush's right end. I used a broad flat brush on rough board.

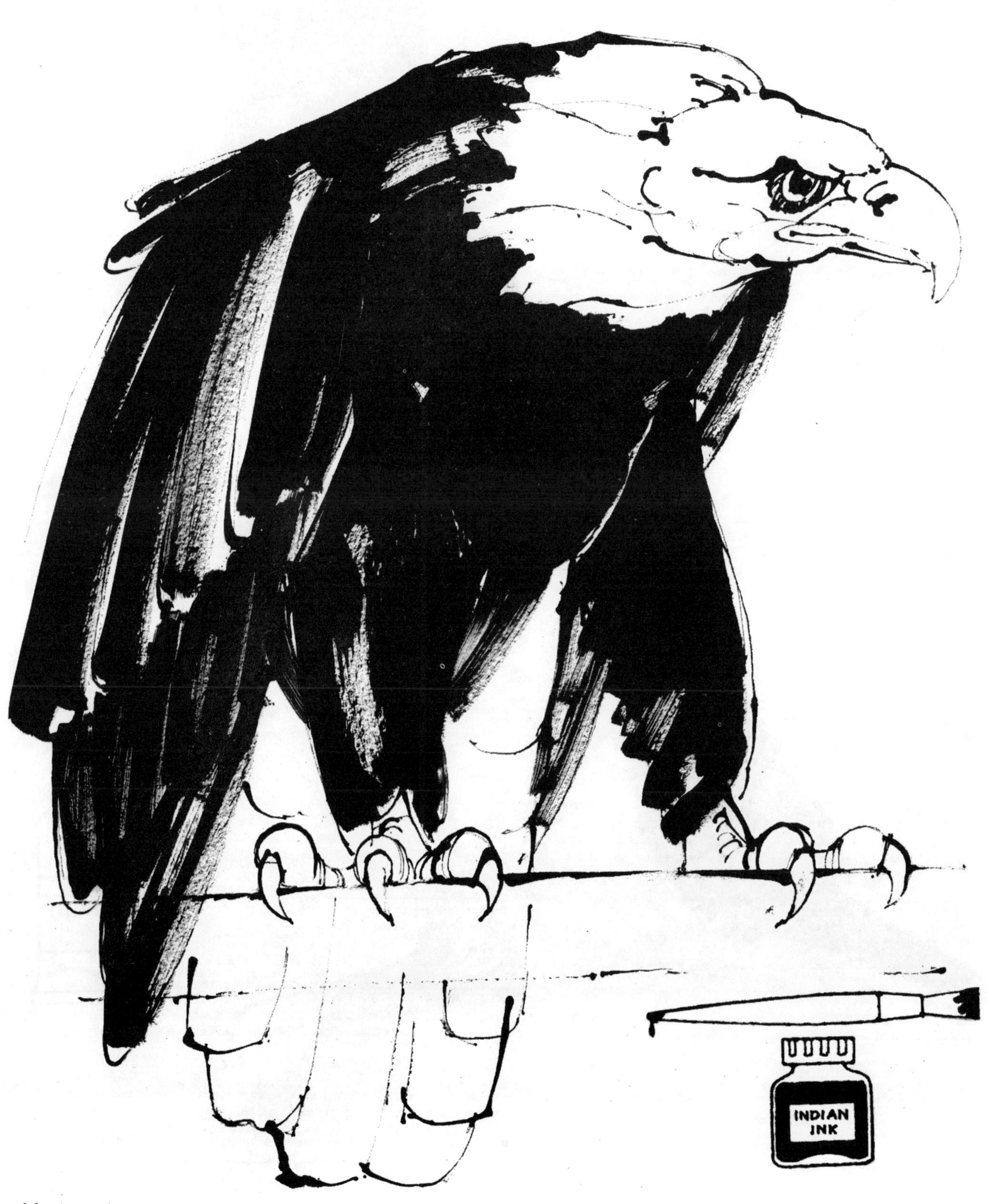

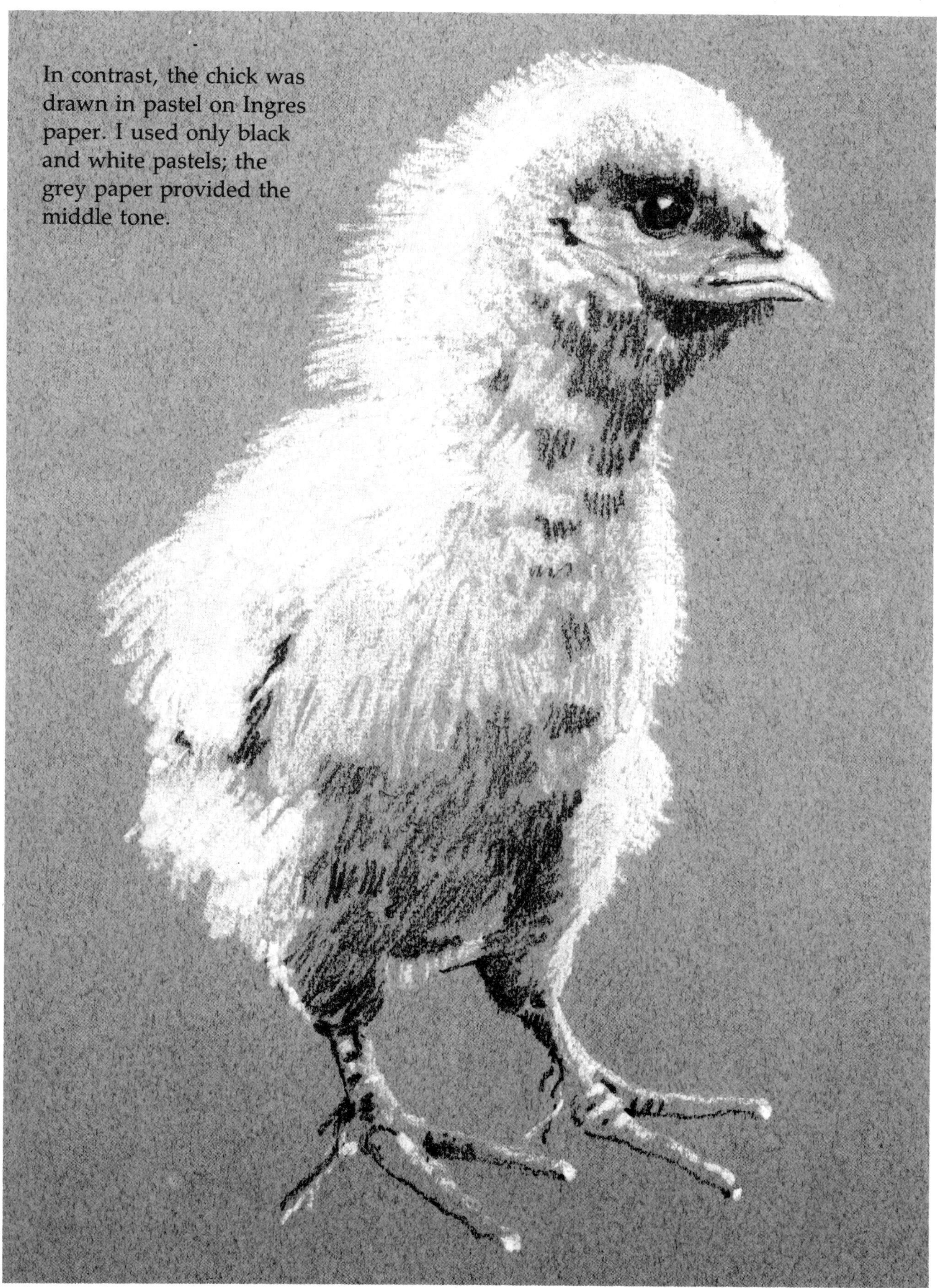

In contrast, the chick was
drawn in pastel on Ingres
paper. I used only black
and white pastels; the
grey paper provided the
middle tone.

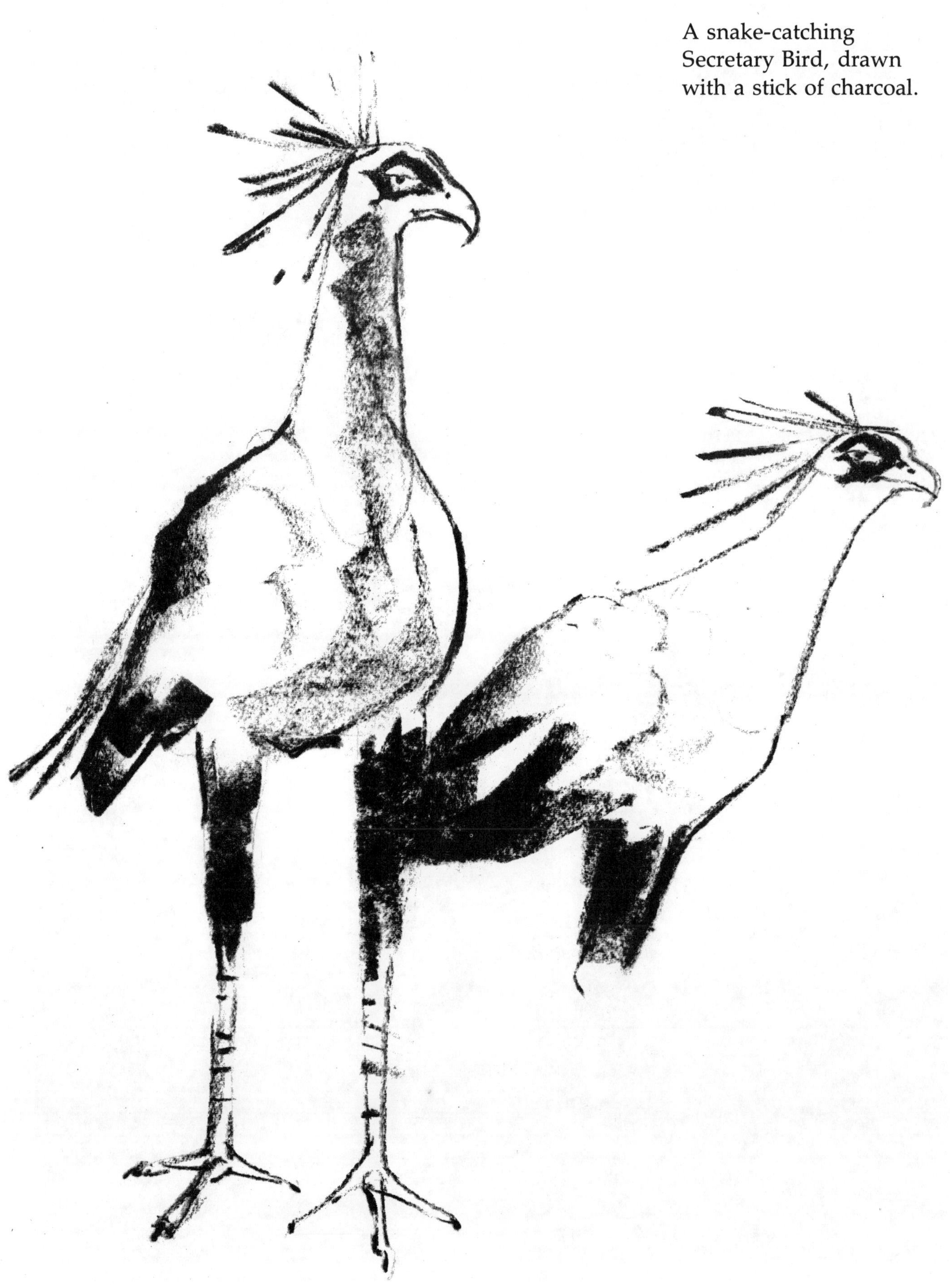

A snake-catching
Secretary Bird, drawn
with a stick of charcoal.